GORGEOUS
Book of
WORD GAME PUZZLES

Gorgeous Book of Word Game Puzzles copyright © 2013 by Andrews McMeel Publishing, LLC. All rights reserved. Puzzles copyright © 2013 by Universal Uclick. All rights reserved. Printed in the United States of America. No part of this book may be used or reproduced in any manner whatsoever without written permission except in the case of reprints in the context of reviews.

Andrews McMeel Publishing, LLC
an Andrews McMeel Universal company
1130 Walnut Street, Kansas City, Missouri 64106

www.andrewsmcmeel.com
www.puzzlesociety.com
www.wonderword.com

13 14 15 16 17 PAH 10 9 8 7 6 5 4 3 2 1

ISBN: 978-1-4494-4820-2

Word Roundup™ by David L. Hoyt and Jeff Knurek
Wonderword puzzles by David Ouellet

This 2013 edition printed exclusively for Barnes & Noble, Inc.

ATTENTION: SCHOOLS AND BUSINESSES
Andrews McMeel books are available at quantity discounts with bulk purchase for educational, business, or sales promotional use. For information, please e-mail the Andrews McMeel Publishing Special Sales Department: specialsales@amuniversal.com

GORGEOUS
Book of
WORD GAME PUZZLES

250 PUZZLES

The
Puzzle Society™
puzzlesociety.com

Andrews McMeel
Publishing, LLC
Kansas City • Sydney • London

WORD ROUNDUP

How to Play

Find the hidden words in the puzzle looking horizontally, vertically, diagonally, backward, and forward. Unlike traditional word searches, Word Roundup gives clues to the words hidden within the puzzles. The words themselves are for solvers to figure out.

1

```
Y X B R O W N D N Z P N
B A B A G F R A N C E L
D F L U U A T H H E G L
N C M E V S X E R Z A E
A U G R E D T G A C S N
L P A B L U E R V L U R
O H C O L U M B I A S O
P R I N C E T O N A V C
```

Find and Circle

Six Ivy League universities	☑○○○○○
Five colors	○○○○○
Three countries that border Germany	○○○
Two drinking vessels	○○
A mythical winged creature	○

2

```
J  V  I  E  N  N  A  Y  A  S  Z  T
L  O  Z  X  E  V  P  P  N  E  N  H
V  L  H  B  K  M  L  E  D  I  I  O
H  K  A  N  U  P  Z  E  R  K  L  M
A  S  C  R  A  B  B  L  E  C  R  A
R  Z  G  X  K  V  E  S  W  O  E  S
R  A  L  P  S  P  R  X  K  R  B  X
Y  M  A  R  T  I  N  Z  R  O  M  E
```

Find and Circle

The first names of six U.S. presidents	✔○○○○○
Four European country capitals	○○○○
Two of Snow White's dwarfs	○○
Two mountain chains	○○
The game invented by Alfred Butts in the 1930s	○

3

```
D I X V K J Z D O H I O
A R N Z J E L B T X B A
I V U D V E N O E Z J R
G J K M I A Z T B O X C
R X A F M A A T U K V T
O C R R K R N L Z C Z I
E A O Z C X J E J X K C
G N M I N N E S O T A Y
```

Find and Circle

Six types of containers	✓○○○○○
Four U.S. states	○○○○
Two oceans	○○
A fictional cat or U.S. president	○
Greg's last name or Rockwell's first name	○

4

```
M C X V S Z E A Z C V N
C A L E O C L G A K A L
Y I L X C O O C Y M H E
P L C I G O I R K P T I
R A H N B S L C P E T N
U M A Z R R A L R I X A
S O D O Z H A C I C O P
C S C V T E R R I E R S
```

Find and Circle

Five African countries	✓○○○○
Three dog breeds	○○○
Three zodiac signs	○○○
Three Mediterranean islands	○○○
Star of *The French Connection*	○

5

```
I  K  N  O  C  K  B  K  X  D  H  Z
X  R  C  O  L  L  A  T  E  R  A  L
V  S  O  V  Z  Y  R  V  E  I  M  X
F  H  P  N  A  E  C  T  G  V  I  K
H  R  X  K  T  K  S  X  D  E  L  C
Z  I  P  T  H  B  I  V  E  R  T  A
P  M  U  V  O  X  H  C  W  Z  O  N
V  P  F  L  F  Z  V  H  K  X  N  K
```

Find and Circle

Four types of golf clubs	✓○○○
Four words that start and end with "K"	○○○○
Three crustaceans	○○○
The capital of Bermuda	○
2004 Tom Cruise movie	○

R C H O C O L A T E H I
L O Z M X V T L T J A J
I H S K O N H L U X E N
L J P E O N V I L N L A
Y V P M K P T N I M A M
G A R D E N I A P U Z U
H E K Z X J M V N M A J
V E R S A T I L E A V H

Find and Circle

Six varieties of flowers	✓○○○○○
Three U.S. states that border Canada	○○○
Two popular flavors of ice cream	○○
The "V" in DVD	○
1995 Robin Williams movie	○

7

C X B C S L E E T J R C
C H I N A E R I E O E O
N U A X W N K Z I H L L
E R C D O F A R D N I O
V O U K N B E D B S H M
E N B I S P K X A O C B
L B A Z U H A I L N X I
E R X S C A M B O D I A

Find and Circle

Seven countries that start with "C"	✓OOOOOO
Four forms of precipitation	OOOO
Three Great Lakes	OOO
Last name of a *Miami Vice* star or a U.S. president	O
The square root of 121	O

```
D O B O E A I S L A N D
E R Z T J F L P J S I Z
T A U S T R A L I A A X
U L Y M O I J L X H T B
L P Z J S C Z A P A N U
F R N A J A S L J R U G
H A R M O N I C A A O L
B H C A N D Y N Z P M E
```

Find and Circle

Nine musical instruments   ✓ O O O O O O O O

Three continents   O O O

Two land formations (no proper names)   O O

The largest desert in the world   O

The name of a funny John who died in 1994   O

9

```
P  J  Z  A  H  A  B  I  S  H  O  P
T  A  G  G  U  H  L  R  O  O  K  G
H  T  W  A  J  S  E  G  H  G  I  Z
G  E  U  N  K  P  T  Y  E  K  N  P
I  N  T  G  P  G  H  R  G  R  G  K
N  O  A  O  Z  A  J  H  I  Y  I  C
K  M  H  L  J  H  W  P  Z  A  C  A
Z  W  J  A  L  B  A  N  I  A  X  Z
```

Find and Circle

Five chess pieces	✓ O O O O
Four countries that start and end with "A"	O O O O
The last name of a French artist who died in 1926	O
The northwest "Four Corners" state	O
A Burger King sandwich	O

10

C J O H N X P O O D L E
O H I O Z V J U X Z R G
V B O X E R C V G A I O
M Y J W H X O P W V N D
O K X P O V L A A J G L
R S V K U J L J X U O L
T U L L N E I Z V V L U
Y H Z X D B E A G L E B

Find and Circle

Nine dogs	✔○○○○○○○○
First names of three Beatles	○○○
Jerry Seinfeld's TV dad	○
The second-smallest U.S. state	○
The state home to the Pro Football Hall of Fame	○

11

```
P Z A T M S O C C E R Y
C I T A P O J R U P B A
A S N N Z P N L E G J R
N I E K G J B T U D Y G
A N G M O O N R A K E R
D N A H L P J K F N J P
A E M Y D Y T E A L A Y
Z T H U N D E R B A L L
```

Find and Circle

Eight colors	✔○○○○○○○
Three sports	○○○
Two James Bond movies	○○
The birthplace of Alex Trebek	○
The Treasure State	○

```
Y Z P V C M I L E E J R
H A C J P O H G C N A E
C P R G E C X C S U N T
E K U D R O W L H J O E
S C H A R J E Z G O Z M
R J M H Y G H K F Z I G
A H N C N A P R I L R H
P G Z A I N C H J M A Y
```

Find and Circle

Six units of length	✓○○○○○
Four consecutive months	○○○○
The last names of three *Friends*	○○○
The southwest "Four Corners" state	○
2002 MLB World Series winner	○

13

```
M Z S O H E V Z N J E E
P A N A L E E P O S A L
R U R Y T G L O T U R L
R U O S D U T P A N T E
E B M I P U R X E E H H
K Z R M L V J N H V J C
O B J P Y A L A S K A I
P Y E S T E R D A Y J M
```

Find and Circle

Five planets	✓○○○○
Four card games	○○○○
The titles of three Beatles songs	○○○
Two *Everybody Loves Raymond* stars	○○
The largest U.S. state	○

14

```
S  Z  K  F  C  H  P  R  D  X  W  A
F  I  P  A  C  R  E  P  N  R  Y  L
S  P  L  T  N  H  E  O  A  A  O  I
A  V  I  K  T  S  T  S  L  Y  M  Y
T  H  F  A  U  T  A  Z  T  O  I  K
I  X  E  E  O  T  V  S  O  N  N  C
N  L  Z  C  L  X  A  P  C  P  G  O
C  O  L  G  A  T  E  H  S  X  K  Z
```

Find and Circle

Six types of materials	✓○○○○○
Three states that border Colorado	○○○
Two Will Smith movies	○○
Two brands of toothpaste	○○
The birthplace of Sean Connery	○

15

```
O Z J D E P P N O R T H
N H E P D A N S O N E N
A R I O W A K B O J N S
I H J O J C L G L Z I A
P A B Z A Z E A H L A S
S T H L X R V J S P M N
A U B L O H B L V K B A
C L Y D E S D A L E A K
```

Find and Circle

Seven U.S. states	✓○○○○○○
Four seas	○○○○
A horse breed	○
The *Cheers* star born in San Diego in 1947	○
An acting Johnny born in Kentucky in 1963	○

```
C G W P N B X G V H X E
D U V E P O A Z T E N N
N T B B S M R R P L A G
A S X A A T O W B F N L
L A Z N B N Z X A Z S A
E E A S C O P E G Y O N
C P T H A I L A N D R D
I L I S T E R I N E B G
```

Find and Circle

Six countries with flags   ✓ ○ ○ ○ ○ ○
   containing red and white

Three directions   ○ ○ ○

Two popular brands of mouthwash   ○ ○

James Bond star born in Ireland   ○

A 2003 Will Ferrell movie   ○

17

```
C X A N G O L A N H F L
A H P J Z R K R K T R I
I H A T L T A L Z N E B
S T Z D P S Y N K O N E
I R K Y E A R Z C M C R
N A G A D X J L L H H I
U E C I S R A E L V J A
T R U S S I A N J X K Z
```

Find and Circle

Five African countries	✓ O O O O
Four kinds of salad dressings	O O O O
Three units of time	O O O
Birthplace of Natalie Portman	O
A planet	O

```
G C D O N K E Y R N Z N
B O I S E Z R C E O I N
L P L B X E E A G T X I
E P P D V S V R I S W U
A E X L R Z G B T O C G
D R I O B V P E C B N N
Z S H I P P O Z N N I E
M A D R I D U M P Z Z P
```

Find and Circle

Six metals	✔○○○○○
Six four-legged mammals	○○○○○○
Two U.S. states capitals that start with "B"	○○
Bird native to Antarctica	○
A European capital	○

19

```
L Z G R A P E F R U I T
B I S P R I T E C T X E
L E M O N H V F O O Y M
I X D E S K O J K Y E D
S F O R D J X N E O N L
P F T A B L E V D T S X
E N I S S A N J F A I F
P T A N G E R I N E D Z
```

Find and Circle

Four citus fruits	✓OOO
Four car companies	OOOO
Three popular soft drink brands	OOO
Three pieces of furniture	OOO
Florida and California theme park developer	O

```
S T O O T S I E Z X D Y
U E V T E G R A N T O Z
R J A L T X J V O J L E
L X A L Z E Z X I V P R
A H O V A L R J T Z H E
W Z C I R C L E A J I H
X R E C T A N G L E N P
O U T B R E A K E Z J S
```

Find **and Circle**

Five marine mammals   ✓○○○○

Three Dustin Hoffman movies   ○○○

Three shapes   ○○○

Two words that refer to positive feelings   ○○

The U.S. president on the $50 bill   ○

21

```
M L S H B E E R H T P H
S I Z L E X Z I A J E W
N A L F E J P F R I X A
O H F K C E W L R P N T
W O E N Z P T E Y R P E
C B H C H E S T E R J R
Z O A N D R E W J C H P
J U I C E V D A F F Y Z
```

Find and Circle

Six drinks	✓OOOOO
Four forms of precipitation	OOOO
The first names of four U.S. presidents	OOOO
A type of gun	O
A fictional duck	O

```
V T W I N S J N X S Z Y
D E L Y D Z U J V N X A
E P R E P O S I T I O N
N E R B N J V X F L P G
V A X Z Y C H E R R Y E
E C E N T R A L R A X L
R H A P P L E X J M J S
A D J E C T I V E N Y Z
```

Find and Circle

Four types of words	⊘○○○
Four professional baseball teams	○○○○
Three types of fruit	○○○
Two U.S. state capitals that start with "D"	○○
Chicago's time zone	○

23

```
U Z F R I D A Y X T B S
X T C K T M A Z N E R A
Y E A N E N O P N K O S
A X A H A R V T X C O N
D A V T Z G M P H I K A
N S N C V C K I V R L K
O O S U N D A Y T C Y X
M V X Z M A R Y L A N D
```

Find and Circle

Five U.S. states	✓OOOO
Three days of the week	OOO
Three insects	OOO
NYC borough, birthplace of Adam Sandler	O
A fictional frog	O

```
J X V Y Z L C U R V E Y
A U P W I N T E R X A O
N Z N R Z G P P A M E C
U J P E N V O Z R Z C T
A A U I T A L Y U V E O
R Y R L F R A N C E E B
Y P X P Y V N P A Y R E
S L I D E R D Z X P G R
```

Find and Circle

Six months	✓○○○○○
Four European countries	○○○○
Two baseball pitches	○○
Two seasons	○○
Division of Honda that makes the Integra	○

25

```
C A U S T I N X G O L F
A O P T Z Y B S V Y G Z
I Z A X V A E O J B N H
G H N T Y O L H Y G I S
R X T J H O T B H U X K
O Z S S P J H Z A R O C
E J E F F E R S O N B O
G S H I R T Z Y J X Y S
```

Find and Circle

Seven things to wear	✓○○○○○○
Four sports	○○○○
Two U.S. state capitals that start with "A"	○○
U.S. president on the $2 bill	○
The largest U.S. state east of the Mississippi	○

```
N C A T C H E R T G X R
Z I G W D O N E B E G E
X D N O R N J G U I N H
N T W E L V E Z C G E C
E X Z G D Z J D K H V T
V T R A V O L T A T E I
E Z D H O U S T O N L P
S H O R T S T O P X E D
```

Find and Circle

Nine numbers	✓○○○○○○○○
Three baseball positions	○○○
Acting John who's also a licensed pilot	○
The largest city in Texas	○
Movie uncle played by John Candy	○

27

E D I M E E B A C O N A
F G Z C L G D A H J D L
L O T G F E R U S G A A A
R F F S A N U A N E C E
D A N W L B T A R J L M
W T R B J V C E V D B T
H O O V E R C L R B J A
F N I X O N P E N N Y O

Find and Circle

Six breakfast items	✓○○○○○
Five U.S. presidents	○○○○○
Three basketball positions	○○○
Two U.S. coins	○○
Country with the greatest number of lakes	○

```
D Z P J R M P F N X P J
H U B A N J O A I E Z K
P J C H J K W L E N R P
Z X L K R S P J L A C L
H P G O O S E Z L U L H
L A T H B A R B I E S J
W S R X I G U I T A R K
O Z J P N T R U C K P X
```

Find and Circle

Eight birds	✓○○○○○○○
Three types of vehicles	○○○
Three stringed instruments	○○○
What a clam or octopus is	○
The name of a popular doll	○

29

```
P Y G J P L E M O N E K
D E G E F E F Z D L C E
R M A N R R A N F M A G
A I P R Z B A C J O R N
W L P G R L I N H U E A
O G L F O A Z L C S B R
H J E P G F T G J E I O
N E C T A R I N E F L Z
```

Find and Circle

Seven types of fruit	✓ ○ ○ ○ ○ ○ ○
Three rodents	○ ○ ○
Two countries that border Germany	○ ○
Flamboyant piano player who died in 1987	○
The director of *A Beautiful Mind*	○

30

```
L A Y J X Z K T D R P O
O Y L B A R P R I E X G
N R N B R C A H R G Z I
T A O X E P K P J G E T
A G I H O R P S K A K R
R U L E Z P T U O J B E
I O L B K L X A M N H V
O C P A N T H E R A B K
```

Find and Circle

Seven felines	✓○○○○○○
Two Canadian provinces	○○
A singing Mick	○
A U.S. state capital	○
A 1958 movie directed by Alfred Hitchcock	○

31

```
T H Z J S N A P P E R Y
Y U S H A R K R B V P A
A R N A B M E E H G Z D
D O T A L P E C R P B S
N N J N U M R S Z I X R
U Z H O B E O H P V E U
S O R H P M O N D A Y H
J G L I V E R P O O L T
```

Find and Circle

Six types of fish	⊘○○○○○
Three days of the week	○○○
The first names of two U.S. presidents	○○
Two Great Lakes	○○
An English port city	○

32

```
L C C Z Y U T O C J Z N
S A K H R J A N U R A L
H N O E I K X E B P A O
R A P S T L I L A K L B
I D Z P U G E J K X A S
M A Y A L K L O J B P T
P G P J Z R R H N V E E
E C U A D O R N Z C N R
```

Find and Circle

Nine countries	✔○○○○○○○○
Three crustaceans	○○○
The first names of two Beatles	○○
Letterman competitor	○
Tony Banta's vehicle	○

33

```
D Y F U A J I O G Y K T
O R L B T G S O B K J E
R J U G A A P I W O N N
E T T M S L H H H A E I
G Y E N Y J P O J P V R
O P A R I S H S Y H A A
N K E L E P H A N T D L
M A N D O L I N E Y A C
```

Find and Circle

Six musical instruments	✔○○○○○
Six U.S. states	○○○○○○
The "City of Light"	○
The largest living land mammal	○
A European mountain chain	○

```
Z K A P H R O D I T E G
E E G Z N F P C M A N F
A A U P G J S A V B G K
P Z S S F H H O B L S T
O N P T T S K V F E J S
L G F U I J B N D A Z E
L N O R M A T L O C K W
O S G P O S E I D O N Y
```

Find and Circle

Four Greek gods/goddesses	✓ O O O
Three directions	O O O
Three pieces of furniture	O O O
Author of *The Firm*	O
A TV lawyer played by Andy Griffith	O

35

```
C Z G Y T J E G J P N A
G U G I S H S U X G I J
N P B D A E A A R S L P
O J E S V N R M A O E Z
Z R Z A Z B T F E P P H
A G R H O G H S G S L E
M B J C P Y T H O N Z P
A N T A R C T I C A J X
```

Find and Circle

Four Major League baseball teams	✓○○○
Three continents	○○○
Two types of snakes	○○
The longest and second-longest rivers	○
The river that runs through London	○

```
P V C M S P R U C E E L
F A L O R A Y P L Z A R
L E L A Y J T G P K R E
O F D M P O O U C H T D
W E O J P O T A R J H W
C N L X G Y J E D N H O
Y I C O L U M B O D F O
J P M A G N O L I A Z D
```

Find and Circle

Seven types of trees   ✓○○○○○○

Four wild canines   ○○○○

Two planets   ○○

A TV detective played by Peter Falk   ○

A popular Internet search engine   ○

37

```
M Z L T D D M C L E R Y
L I N C H C T O T E G F
E A L N K N S I T L N O
N B K E O U M E D H O O
I H E M N R M C H K L T
A F R E E D N A N D R C
M E V T Z C F B R K U D
V C R I C K E T G S F Z
```

Find and Circle

Five units of length	✓○○○○
Five insects	○○○○○
Two New England states	○○
The Roman goddess of love and beauty	○
The Roman god of war	○

```
P X J Z W B C J B J V X
B E K H E H R W L P A N
X F R L N H A A Z A I O
J B I U G G E L Z C V O
Z H J D L S H R E I I T
C X H D A B N U J F L A
N I X O N J Z S K I O L
E C U A D O R X K C B P
```

Find and Circle

Five South American countries	✓OOOO
Three marine mammals	OOO
Three movies directed by Oliver Stone	OOO
Bob Hope's birthplace	O
San Francisco's time zone	O

39

```
P A F F L E C K D V Y R
D O Z T T A F T N X E Y
R H L N Y G F Z A L L Z
O Y A K J I C J L X S N
F R C Y O B E I E B G O
G J X G E C T R C J N X
Z A D A M S Z B I X I I
D I S N E Y L A N D K N
```

Find and Circle

Eight U.S. presidents

Three popular actors named Ben

Walt's amusement park that opened in 1955

North Atlantic island country

Sport played by Tiger and Phil

```
F Z S N R S T C H Y F E
E O E I G O L H Z E N P
V T U Y X L S A E O A Y
I J W R D N E E C L Z T
F E P O E X F A H K V E
X A D V O D P F S C S N
F N E V I O L E T O X I
Z S H O R T S C Z Y N N
```

Find and Circle

Eight numbers	✓○○○○○○○
Three styles of pants	○○○
Two flowers	○○
A Pacino and De Niro movie	○
The last name of a Jackie who died in 1987	○

41

A Z B F A T H E R Y I J
Y U A O X P A T T O N S
H M N U S J U P P V D I
E O I T S T X R S Z I S
S T E L J T O M P H G T
I H C O U S I N G L O E
O E E X L R Z N W P E R
B R Z J C J G A N D H I

Find and Circle

Seven relatives	✓ O O O O O O
Three U.S. state capitals	O O O
Two colors	O O
Mohandas or Indira	O
WWII general named George	O

```
N Y X J U N E T R A I N
D E S J O C H I N A W E
D M O D W C A L D O A G
Y K A N A K I Y N X I O
L R R Y G R L S P D S R
P D K J P S L E E T S T
X J C A N O E G J Y U I
K H E L I U M X P K R N
```

Find and Circle

Four gases	✓○○○
Four forms of precipitation	○○○○
Three types of boat	○○○
Three months	○○○
The two countries that border Mongolia	○○

43

```
K O Y S T E R C R O O K
H I Z C Y K P P L D Z H
S G N P G N O N X A P S
I P H G I I H E Y L M I
N C A T C G S W C L H L
A Y A W J H I M G A Z G
P L Z P N T B A X S K N
S C A L L O P N Z K Y E
```

Find and Circle

Five chess pieces	✓○○○○
Three languages	○○○
Three mollusks	○○○
The name of a sitcom mailman	○
A top-rated TV show set in Texas	○

```
L M O O L A H C B Z P T
L O C E A N P L A P X E
H A O Z F F L G Y S L N
G P K T X E G Z H L H N
U O Y E S O C C E R X I
O N X S Y P Z H F Y H S
D D U S P I E L B E R G
B R E A D L A G O O N Z
```

Find and Circle

Five words that mean "money"	✓○○○○
Five bodies of water (no proper names)	○○○○○
Two sports	○○
The director of *Saving Private Ryan*	○
The last name of a Kurt born in 1951	○

45

M E D I S O N Z F D P H
H U X D E E R L H N I S
O C L P A G O X K A S A
R P A E R W O Z F L T J
S I W M B R F A P T O A
E O F X E L J H T O L K
C Z H L Z L P C P C K G
M U S K E T Z H F S Y Z

Find and Circle

Eight four-legged mammals   ✓ O O O O O O O

Three types of guns   O O O

An inventor who had more than 1,000 patents   O

United Kingdom country   O

The last name of a popular game show host   O

```
M T O V J U P I T E R P
E A P A E M X K P E M N
R D R F H N A P N D O E
C E L S R U U U X J L H
U N P U G L T S I P O C
R F T X J P D L D P K T
Y A C H E Y E N N E A I
S P Y N C A L I C O I K
```

Find and Circle

Six planets   ✔ ○ ○ ○ ○ ○

Three Hawaiian islands   ○ ○ ○

Two rooms commonly found in a house   ○ ○

The capital of Wyoming   ○

A blotched or spotted cat   ○

47

U Z A V X O T J U N E E
A T J P H C P E U P B R
N E A A P B E E X L V A
A M D H R L Y V A A Y W
T I J A I A E J N C S A
N L E N M X M A R C H L
O P A A C A P U L C O E
M Z W Y O M I N G Z Y D

Find and Circle

Six U.S. states	✓○○○○○
Four fruits	○○○○
Four months	○○○○
A Mexican seaside resort	○
The world's longest river	○

48

```
F G W M O T H R H W N S
A E O E Z X A Y A A A W
S A T U E D V J R S C I
I N B A D K Y D V P I S
A T Z E J A E D A J R S
G V H Y E H L N R X E Z
O C O S T N E R D P M V
L I M B U R G E R Z A X
```

Find and Circle

Seven types of cheese	✓○○○○○○
Four insects	○○○○
The Guardian star	○
A two-day time period	○
Prestigious Massachusetts university	○

49

```
R G Y P K Z G M J R A P
N O R T H G K O P A O Z
S S C P Y Z P N G P Z G
E P G K F R I D A Y K Z
U E K S U N D A Y P C T
L L Z P J Z P Y H K O S
B P E N I N S U L A P A
C L A S S I C A L Y S E
```

Find and Circle

Seven styles of music	✓ ○ ○ ○ ○ ○ ○
Three days of the week	○ ○ ○
Two directions	○ ○
What most of Florida is	○
A popular *Star Trek* character	○

```
S X O W L B A P D L P S
S W N B E A R M Y U U P
B T A S C R B N L R C P
L O O N Y I I Z U D R K
N O B R P E L A C I A Y
G L E O K S T Y C N N V
M I N N E S O T A G E A
A L B A T R O S S O P N
```

Find and Circle

Eight types of birds ⊘ O O O O O O O

Four signs of the zodiac O O O O

Two branches of the U.S. armed services O O

The setting for *Little House On the Prairie* (TV) O

An Australian dog O

51

```
C D O V E R T A N Z K Z
N Y H C I N Y B L U E N N
N S A L E O P Y L R P D
E A R N Y L L L M A I E
E L P A P N L I O E E T
R E D Z H U R O N Y R I
G M A L B A N Y T P R H
N V I O L E T Z H N E W
```

Find and Circle

Seven colors	✓oooooo
Four U.S. state capitals	oooo
Three stringed instruments	ooo
Three units of duration	ooo
A Great Lake	o

52

```
B P W M O U S E Z R C J
K E R O O S E V E L T Z
L A A M L P J E C P A J
O D S R O F D Y R N F N
P R Z I H O R S E O T O
C O U G A R S J I X P I
A F R I C A Z E P I Z L
T R A N S Y L V A N I A
```

Find and Circle

Eight four-legged mammals ✓○○○○○○○

The last names of six U.S. presidents ○○○○○○

Two continents ○○

Famous Romanian region ○

A large feline ○

53

```
D C S A X O P H O N E T
Z R P U G B C P E R U E
F L U T E R A L Z R V N
E C V M A L G N V E E I
O Z H T H A Z P J X D R
B C I O E K L L C O Y A
O U V B W Z H X V B L L
G V P A M P L O N A C C
```

Find and Circle

Seven musical instruments	✓○○○○○○
Four breeds of dog	○○○○
Home to the Running of the Bulls	○
Bonnie Parker's partner	○
A country on the Pacific Ocean	○

```
I  J  H  E  V  T  I  N  Y  J  X  P
P  N  L  A  W  I  I  P  T  A  E  V
H  I  C  O  W  A  R  E  X  P  R  J
M  A  N  H  R  K  E  O  R  V  U  D
E  S  I  G  J  L  X  D  N  B  T  L
T  J  V  L  S  G  K  L  V  K  L  E
E  S  U  B  W  A  Y  O  P  X  U  A
R  F  O  O  T  E  A  G  L  E  V  D
```

Find and Circle

Five units of length	✓○○○○
Four forms of precipitation	○○○○
Four metals	○○○○
Three birds of prey	○○○
A restaurant chain with more than 25,000 locations	○

55

```
L O T T A W A A M Z B R
T I A X A S E D I U X O
U R L B I L P M A R M S
L Z U Y A N C A O I A E
I C K Z P B D X I U S N
P B A G E R B I L N S Y
A R C H I P E L A G O E
H I B I S C U S B C Z P
```

Find and Circle

Seven flowers	✓○○○○○○
Four countries	○○○○
Three rodents	○○○
What Indonesia is	○
The capital of Canada	○

```
P L A T I N S O C C E R
H O C K E Y G C G R H X
G R L R X N I P P Y S L
Y U Y O I B X G X L I G
B T G X A W A L E S D F
G H O R F R E N C H E L
U B A I T A L I A N W O
R T E N N I S E A L S G
```

Find and Circle

Seven sports	✓○○○○○○
Five languages	○○○○○
Part of the United Kingdom	○
Yankee slugger who died in 1948	○
A marine mammal	○

57

```
P T U R T L E P H V M Z
S I P Z C P T C Z S A L
N H N A D E R A E B G I
A P M E L I D M N E N Z
K L R V B M A A Z I O A
E G R A Y J H O R G L R
B R O W N E L L A E I D
A L L I G A T O R K A P
```

Find and Circle

Seven types of trees	✓oooooo
Four reptiles	oooo
Four colors	oooo
The "B" in Susan B. Anthony	o
Novelist Henry	o

```
Y J P M D J L Y K D L Y
P E R S K E A H V L A P
D O A E P D C W K D F Y
N P E R N I N A S J R M
O W K O N P N E D V I O
C V M U V K U A N E D N
E A M I S T A D C L A T
S C E N T U R Y J H Y H
```

Find and Circle

Seven units of duration	✓○○○○○○
Three days of the week	○○○
Three movies directed by Steven Spielberg	○○○
Popeye's leafy vegetable	○
Popular character played by George Wendt	○

59

F P X T H R E E Y T P G
G I G C P N E C L T W Z
S C V Z D N I Y L R H O
N R C E I G N C E A T Y
Z A F N M N K P K W U T
O B N F E D G Z L E E F
L N C P D Z L P N T L I
E L E V E N Z N P S S F

Find and Circle

Eight numbers ✔○○○○○○○

Three coins ○○○

Rear Window stars ○○

Sherlock Holmes is one ○

Blue, horseshoe or fiddler_____ ○

60

```
J L D N L Y T H Z N P M
H U O R L O R E I L A A
Z R N U I E N L X H R R
I L J E T V R D V A I C
Y H L T Z E E L O P S H
A V U B B H L R V N R L
M P O C T O B E R R H V
F L E M I N G Z R O M E
```

Find and Circle

Five months	✓ O O O O
Four European capitals	O O O O
Three golf clubs ("wedge," for example)	O O O
James Bond creator	O
Lone Star State	O

61

```
P C A P R I C O T R H L
L E C G H P N K A P C E
U L A T I N E L H O Y M
M K G R M E L S R U R O
G H E U R O G R O N R N
C K N G D K O C H D E V
O R A N G E P S C K H C
H P E A C H F R E N C H
```

Find and Circle

Seven varieties of fruit	✓○○○○○○
Four units of currency	○○○○
Three languages	○○○
The largest member of the deer family	○
Acting Nicolas born in 1964	○

62

```
H C Z C D E N V E R T N
N I A P L Y H G H B R I
U X L N E I R X R E E A
O P H L Y O F E E T N T
N X L Z G O V F T O T N
R A V I N E N X S Y O U
V A U S T I N H Y O N O
I S L A N D P Z O C H M
```

Find and Circle

Eight land formations (no proper names)	✓ O O O O O O O
Three U.S. state capitals	O O O
Two types of words ("adjective," for example)	O O
A wolf-like canine	O
A pearl producer	O

63

O H I M P A L A Z Y B C
C H Z C A L A S K A R O
M A I N E D K C H T O L
E C Z O I N Y D X N O O
U H C R I M S O N E K R
L D O P C R X H T G L A
B L R E I N E R C A Y D
F K A N S A S D H M N O

Find and Circle

Six U.S. states	✓○○○○○
Six colors	○○○○○○
A N.Y.C. borough	○
A type of antelope	○
Carl, or his son Rob	○

```
L G J L O C E A N T L F
H A V O K C L Z I W O L
T E K R N X R A G H N U
I S O E L E R O R A D G
M T V R X T S P W L O D
S X L G S V R G R E N Y
E D O L E N Z R X O A G
N L A G O O N G P B V L
```

Find and Circle

Eight bodies of water (no proper names) ✓ O O O O O O O

The last names of The Monkees O O O O

Birthplace of Elizabeth Taylor O

Killer or blue _____ O

Acting Russell born in New Zealand in 1964 O

65

```
L M O N G O L I A P Z N
Z A V C A P I S C E S E
L E O I Z A S P B C S P
C C D S R E H X O Y U A
H N P B I G Z V X A R L
I C I R V P O C I L U P
N L A O A K L A N D A H
A V I E T N A M G A T Z
```

Find and Circle

Six countries	✓○○○○○
Six signs of the zodiac	○○○○○○
A city on San Francisco Bay	○
Cinderella Man sport	○
M*A*S*H star born in 1936	○

```
A S I S T E R H M C M L
P U N M A R S O I O O E
C O N N Z W H O N L T F
S O O T E E L V E U H F
Z I U H P L B E R M E A
L X P S O G P R V B R R
K E K P I P H G A U X I
N G A V E N U S B S H G
```

Find and Circle

Six relatives	✔○○○○○
Four Roman gods	○○○○
An exploring Christopher	○
The tallest animal	○
_____ Dam	○

67

O C W L X F I D D L E T
J B X E T H E L Z R B R
G H O R L T J R H X U U
P O E E I L H O N J G M
R B N M H Z S H N I L P
A L R Z X P P K X E E E
H E L J O B A C K U S T
K T R O M B O N E J L Z

Find and Circle

Seven musical instruments   ✓○○○○○○

Four Muppet characters   ○○○○

The Jim who voiced Mr. Magoo   ○

Dean, Davy or Tom _____   ○

The author of *The Time Machine*   ○

```
P H I L A D E L P H I A
Z I S A L M O N S D J P
L S K G R A N T R O R Y
A H Y E F Z Y O R A C E
D A P O L K F J C O O K
N R H A L I B U T H U J
A K R O B E R T S Z P T
S F S N E A K E R F J Y
```

Find and Circle

Six types of fish	⊘○○○○○
Four things you wear on your foot	○○○○
Three U.S. presidents	○○○
A 1993 Tom Hanks movie	○
An acting Julia born in 1967	○

69

```
G Y P K A T E A L H B Z
Z O N A I L H Z X N I H
R I L G W N A G H I S W
P O G D S N G S Y T H O
D Y O T P P Z H K R O L
E T E K B I L L S A P L
R J A K N I G H T M G E
O R A N G E B E A R S Y
```

Find and Circle

Seven colors	⊘ O O O O O O
Five chess pieces	O O O O O
Three NFL teams	O O O
The first name of the director of *Goodfellas*	O
Home to the highest point in North America	O

70

```
N P Z N I T R O G E N P
J E P G O F L I C K A Z
C H O Y Z R J H A M T N
P U R N T H T R P L I O
N X B N R H B H A I O L
O R U A J O O E E F N Y
O O P Z C Z T N Y R U N
N E U T R O N Z J K N Z
```

Find and Circle

Nine words that begin
  and end with "N"   ✓ ○ ○ ○ ○ ○ ○ ○ ○

Two types of snakes   ○ ○

Two words that mean "movie"   ○ ○

A greenish-blue color   ○

The birthplace of Andy Garcia   ○

71

```
G P E T A L S P G Z M T
C O W P P M F O E U A G
H P A E F L D M T C I L
C L M T H K E N R P K E
O A H E Z K E A F R A T
O T M R C M P P T M T S
M E Z E O M U L E S A A
S S P M S T A P L E B P
```

Find and Circle

Eight mammals   ✓○○○○○○○

Five words that A-E-L-P-S-T unscramble into   ○○○○○

Two words that mean "kiss"   ○○

An eight-letter word that begins and ends with "M"   ○

_____ Jennings, Sellers or Benchley   ○

72

```
H M O W L N P W P Z P P
T A Z P I P H E R O E E
O Y W B U T U T E E P N
R Y O K R P S M A P N G
R R P O C A R B P R K U
A I N Z E C A O R O Z I
P U L P Y P M N I P C N
O R I O L E P D L A R K
```

Find and Circle

Eight birds	✔○○○○○○○
Eight words that begin and end with "P"	○○○○○○○○
Two directions	○○
Two months	○○
A planet	○

73

```
R Z S L E E T A F P P W
G A D P M I S T G V O G
P E I N X R Y N Z N H P
B P X N I N I A S L C P
K G F A A A X L V F K H
S P H B W P Z T G L R A
E C L T P G P A L Z O I
D A N N A P O L I S P L
```

Find and Circle

Five forms of precipitation   ☑ ○ ○ ○ ○

Three U.S. state capitals that start with "A"   ○ ○ ○

Three pieces of furniture   ○ ○ ○

A cut of meat that begins and ends with "P"   ○

Author Mark who died in 1910   ○

```
B J S P A R M E S A N J
L L P W Y B L A B Z B R
U E U B I B X B J P A I
R M L E U S O F Z O T C
B O V F P L S O G F H O
C N L P B Z B N N J T T
P R O V O L O N E E U T
B I B J Z C F P P J B A
```

Find and Circle

Six types of cheese	✔ ○ ○ ○ ○ ○
Six words that begin and end with "B"	○ ○ ○ ○ ○ ○
A citrus fruit	○
A U.S. frontiersman who died in 1820	○
A large African river or a 1995 movie	○

75

```
C M D L T O G O F O Z D
L U O B O E L A N I P X
X P B T C R T A N Z J P
D H E A H E I U E T X I
A A Z R N P X E B V D R
H R X R U P B Z C A B A
C P O R T U G U E S E N
D H L A O S D L U N C H
```

Find and Circle

Seven countries with four-letter names	✓○○○○○○
Four insects	○○○○
Four musical instruments	○○○○
Two meals	○○
A language	○

R V S K I F F L P L Y K
C A R K G X S D Z I A A
C X F N B E E C F V C Y
A E U T G R S H A E H A
N L D R C U A F E R T K
O Z A A E F Z I J A E P
E B S Z R X J P N Z R D
F E R R Y S G A T E S T

Find and Circle

Eight types of boats	✓○○○○○○○
Four human organs	○○○○
Three words that A-E-C-D-R-S unscramble into	○○○
A wealthy Bill born in 1955	○
A Greek god, the son and successor of Kronos	○

77

```
M J A E L P R A F O O T
F I P R D E Y L S L P I
U A L R T E U M E I K N
R L A E K H H R I M A C
L Y M N F P U L O A U H
O B O S T O N R G P M R
N M B A L T I M O R E I
G P A R S E C P K J K P
```

Find and Circle

Seven units of length	✓○○○○○○
Three large U.S. east coast cities	○○○
Three primates	○○○
Two continents	○○
The name of a popular Dudley Moore movie	○

```
P E A P P L E L X N H J
W L C I V I C S E P E O
R G U N P X C V W M R R
E G O M O L A O D A O A
N O X G P R R K M J N N
L B N C O C O O N I P G
M A G P I E C Y N I C E
M S T R A W B E R R Y X
```

Find and Circle

Six varieties of fruit	✓ ○ ○ ○ ○ ○
Six types of birds	○ ○ ○ ○ ○ ○
Three words that begin and end with "C"	○ ○ ○
A 1985 movie directed by Ron Howard	○
A word game from Hasbro	○

79

```
N D E I G H T C D S A D
X I M C Z V E R B A N A
Q A N R O V N T N L G D
H E U E L U N C I A O F
D O N E O U S M X M L I
F O W N A Z D I O I O F
S T H I R T E E N M B T
S E V E N T U R K E Y Y
```

Find and Circle

Eight numbers	✔ooooooo
Five relatives	ooooo
Four deli meats	oooo
Two types of words	oo
A U.S. president	o

```
P E T A F T W O W D A K
T O R E C L I E R K D P
P R L W I N D O W C A N
N N U K A S F O I O M E
O O X M E K D G L L S H
L M M Y A I X O L L P P
O O A X W N K L O O J Y
C H P E R I O D W P G H
```

Find and Circle

Seven U.S. presidents	✔○○○○○○
Four words that begin and end with "W"	○○○○
Four punctuation marks	○○○○
An artist portrayed by Ed Harris	○
A deep yellowish color	○

81

```
P A S P E N T E S H Z H
S A Z M H L Y L U A P E
P X L C A E L T N M W M
O E R M L I M T E M R L
H I H R R P L A V E E O
B S A D Z X H E R R N C
A B P L I E R S P S C K
S Y C A M O R E Z H H X
```

Find and Circle

Seven types of trees   ✓○○○○○○

Five hand tools   ○○○○○

Three common beer ingredients   ○○○

Two planets   ○○

The largest city on Puget Sound   ○

```
R F L L D I A M O N D E
F U A I G T A H S F C R
F P B K B L I E E O R I
O E N Y U R C B N R E H
L N M B E S A Z I W T P
E H I U I A N H D A N P
O F X P R X R Z O R E A
E M E R A L D P I D C S
```

Find and Circle

Five birthstones	✓○○○○
Three human bones	○○○
Three signs of the zodiac	○○○
Two basketball positions	○○
Wyatt played by Kevin Costner	○

83

J P E A C H M S U L J D
D U L O O T L A P R I L
Y M N X D H E I R O X S
T A P E W L P C M C C Z
T Y X U P E D H A E H K
O L L P H S X N S P J
C U A U G U S T G J H D
S J K I R K G D O U G H

Find and Circle

Six months	✓○○○○○
Four fruits	○○○○
Four classic *Star Trek* characters	○○○○
Three words that mean "money"	○○○
A direction	○

```
I D P O U N D W A L T Z
N O E K I N G N C D J P
O L W L P S O A P D K O
G L D A A R K P J C S O
E A J S U W D A A E G H
R R N E D E A J P N N I
O A D E U C E R A K E O
K S A L S A J T E Z Y P
```

Find and Circle

Five U.S. states	✓○○○○
Five units of currency	○○○○○
Four playing cards	○○○○
Three dances	○○○
A country in the Far East	○

85

```
I  U  R  A  N  I  U  M  X  T  P  J
L  R  V  O  D  M  P  C  R  R  I  X
E  R  O  D  N  O  O  E  J  O  R  N
B  R  A  N  P  T  V  U  N  C  E  O
X  E  I  T  R  A  A  E  S  K  P  R
L  V  L  E  E  A  L  X  R  E  P  U
L  J  V  B  B  X  P  L  I  V  O  H
P  L  A  T  I  K  U  J  J  B  C  J
```

Find and Circle

Five metals	✓○○○○
Three rodents	○○○
Three styles of music	○○○
Two Great Lakes	○○
A U.S. state capital	○

```
G E A R N E S T J G R H
N O N E A R E S T E I J
R P N P H M N L G Z O G
E G A G I O P I I P R N
T N J L M H T U P O A I
S I H E A B D O M E N V
A O L J A G U A R A G I
E G L O W I N G P J E G
```

Find and Circle

Six words that begin and end with "G"	✓○○○○○
Four cats	○○○○
Three words that A-E-E-N-R-S-T unscramble to	○○○
Three citrus fruits	○○○
Home to your stomach	○

87

```
C Z G B S K I T T E N E
D A U E Y T E F P L C L
M C L P N T O D L A O I
F A P A E L P T R L N
B U J V Z E R S E I O T
P K I O I V O A L M N L
C R L Y R L X F L D E O
P I G L E T B P N A L C
```

Find and Circle

Six young animal names	✓OOOOO
Five military ranks	OOOOO
Two common street signs	OO
A river that flows into the Mediterranean	O
Popular ABC show produced J.J. Abrams	O

88

```
S P A I N R P Z Y O R D
N O L A O S C E I X E P
R C F E M U R H R B S A
E J H A C I O W A U S C
T C F I B U L A T I E I
S M A I N E X T A J R F
A T I B I A V L P H D I
E C E N T R A L B D G C
```

Find and Circle

Four pieces of furniture	✔○○○
Four countries	○○○○
Three time zones	○○○
Three human bones	○○○
Three U.S. states	○○○

89

O Z B E R L I N Y D C K
J S F X C V P R A F T E
C E L E V A W P O V X J
L T I O R O N O T M C L
U H M X C R M O O S E I
O E A S J C Y L E Z B N
E L O N D O N S B O T V
S M S A H A R A G C X P

Find and Circle

Seven country capitals   ✓ O O O O O O

Four types of boats   O O O O

Two deserts   O O

Large member of the deer family   O

Lucy Ricardo's pal   O

90

```
J Z R S M G X D G M H Y
H U B E B E Z B N D A G
A U N Y D A T H B A W Y
C P L E K S G S H F A S
X U R S Z U D G H F I N
J H A I A J H D Z Y I I
G L X V L A N G E L S W
A A U G U S T Z G X H T
```

Find and Circle

Five months	✓○○○○
Five Major League baseball teams	○○○○○
The last two U.S. states admitted to the Union	○○
Acting Vince born in Minnesota in 1970	○
A cartoon duck	○

91

```
I  L  Z  K  U  W  A  I  T  C  Y  L
A  R  I  N  B  C  Z  R  I  X  P  I
L  Y  A  L  I  G  A  N  O  I  D  B
I  S  M  N  Y  G  A  I  L  S  D  Y
E  I  A  V  C  T  E  U  N  V  E  A
N  A  Z  B  I  Z  T  R  D  E  G  B
S  D  O  T  Y  X  B  C  I  F  C  Y
Z  I  N  D  O  N  E  S  I  A  Z  C
```

Find and Circle

Five OPEC countries	✓○○○○
Four flowers	○○○○
Two movies directed by James Cameron	○○
Acting Michael born in England in 1933	○
Long river that flows into the Atlantic	○

```
B  S  I  L  V  E  R  I  G  R  N  I
O  L  B  T  I  N  T  E  R  I  E  N
R  I  U  C  Z  E  S  R  E  O  Y  D
A  B  G  E  L  N  D  A  E  M  N  I
N  R  C  O  I  L  G  S  N  A  L  G
G  A  I  W  L  H  K  E  Z  C  E  O
E  V  T  N  P  D  J  R  C  A  A  D
Z  I  N  C  Y  E  L  L  O  W  D  Z
```

Find and Circle

Seven colors of the spectrum ⬤○○○○○○

Six metals ○○○○○○

Two Arnold Schwarzenegger movies ○○

The seventh sign of the zodiac ○

Large, long-tailed parrot ○

93

```
P D Y F R A N C Y L F T
D E C I R C L E A E O E
O D S H N E B V X O N Z
L R J O L C O O F I R E
L A V B E N H H N D E E
A Y U X L V X Y V D T P
R R T R I A N G L E E U
E U R O M P H J X D M R
```

Find and Circle

Seven currencies	✔○○○○○○
Five units of length	○○○○○
Three shapes	○○○
Character created by Ian Fleming	○
The square root of 81	○

```
L B D L A N E E S B C A
C A N I F Z K V T E B O
Y I K L M I Y S S U A C
P D U E R P Z X C R R E
L G F T I N L E T O Z A
B J S L I M P E D P R N
K A E R O S M I T H N E
Z H Y S P A R E P O N D
```

Find and Circle

Seven bodies of water (no proper names) ✓ ○ ○ ○ ○ ○ ○

Five words related to bowling ○ ○ ○ ○ ○

Two words that D-E-I-L-M-P unscramble to ○ ○

Island about 90 miles south of Florida ○

Steven Tyler's rock band ○

95

```
F Z Y B R O D Y B Z H H
V O M A D O N N A S S O
C H X N R G P H U E H F
G R N X S H Z H M L U F
Z E O F T G N L A A T M
P B D W Y I O J K H C A
H A S H E H Z L B W H N
W A S H I N G T O N Z Y
```

Find and Circle

Six recent "Best Actor" winners (2000-2005)	✔︎○○○○○
Five words that begin and end with "H"	○○○○○
Character created by Sir Arthur Conan Doyle	○
Largest mammal	○
_____ Louise Ciccone (singer/actress)	○

```
H B Z T H E R O N Y R Y
K A E L K I D M A N O Z
J G W R R K W N T N B K
D O O K R O D C L E E N
M H J O R Y B I A P R A
Y G T C S F D I M V T W
N S G A T E S Z N E S S
W I T H E R S P O O N Y
```

Find and Circle

Six birds	✔○○○○○
Six recent "Best Actress" winners (2000-2005)	○○○○○○
Two coins	○○
A Bill who dropped out of Harvard	○
A Mediterranean island	○

97

```
D C T P U M A Z M L P E
M E A R S P L N G E O L
A B E R U N R Y E O G U
K N E R I C O J N K A M
E J T A T S K W I X C T
R B R Z R Z X J A H I D
H F A N T A S I A F H C
S M O L E S L E E T C B
```

Find and Circle

Seven mammals with four-letter names	✓○○○○○○
Three types of vehicles	○○○
Three forms of precipitation	○○○
Three popular animated movies	○○○
The birthplace of Robin Williams	○

```
L V J N C O X L P M H N
B I V A G A T R U E A J
C D M N C V S P N C A H
H B A E N K X H E K A R
C M C N L I S P E J P S
A L M O N D X O G W P X
E V P O D V F O N H L V
P T A N G E R I N E E G
```

Find and Circle

Six fruits	✓○○○○○
Three nuts	○○○
Three U.S. presidents	○○○
The director/writer of *Star Wars*	○
A time of day	○

99

```
K B O X I N G S T E E L
Z I S H I C O M Y Z U A
F Y N A B A A R F J R G
R A W G M H F R M H O U
A T S J S C D R L G P T
N Z Z I V T P N I A E R
C Y R X A R Z L K C Y O
E G C R I C H T O N A P
```

Find and Circle

Five famous authors	✓○○○○
Three *Cheers* characters	○○○
Three continents	○○○
Two countries that border Spain	○○
A sport	○

```
C V T Z R C A N A D A Z
G U D I E O X Y I P N C
N F B L T B O P D A H H
I B I A R A S K O W S I
K H C A C U N H B N I N
C J L D C F G X M L N A
C O L O M B I A A K A X
M I N C I S O R C J D D
```

Find and Circle

Six countries that start with "C"	✔︎○○○○○
Three types of teeth	○○○
Three chess pieces	○○○
A language or a pastry	○
Saturn's largest moon	○

WONDERWORD

How to Play

First, read the list of words, then look at the puzzle. The words are found in all directions—vertically, horizontally, diagonally, backward. Circle each letter of a word found and strike it off the list. The letters are often used more than once, so do not cross them out. It is best to find the big words first. When you find all the words listed in the clues, you'll have a number of letters left over that spell out the WONDERWORD™.

101

A Day at Work

Solution: 6 letters

C	K	E	X	P	E	R	I	E	N	C	E	D	S	Y
O	C	O	S	N	E	D	S	K	N	A	B	C	R	K
P	A	E	O	R	O	R	E	E	U	I	H	A	R	G
S	R	D	E	C	U	C	S	E	R	E	T	E	T	N
D	E	O	T	Y	I	N	C	O	D	O	L	U	I	I
G	E	O	F	F	O	A	F	U	N	C	T	I	O	N
N	R	N	F	E	L	L	L	E	P	N	I	S	D	R
I	I	O	T	P	S	E	P	S	E	A	E	T	A	A
D	E	A	K	I	B	S	R	M	S	R	T	L	Y	E
R	M	R	G	T	S	U	I	K	E	E	W	I	S	C
A	O	T	I	A	O	T	S	O	P	P	R	S	O	O
W	V	S	L	H	R	O	E	Y	N	A	H	T	T	N
E	E	A	G	E	N	T	L	M	A	I	D	E	S	O
R	R	E	V	I	R	D	L	S	F	R	E	S	A	M
Y	N	O	I	T	A	V	I	T	O	M	R	I	F	Y

AGENT, ARTS, BANK, BUSY, CAREER, CITY, CLERK, COOK, COPS,
DAYS, DENTIST, DOCTOR, DONE, DRIVER, EARNING, ECONOMY,
EMPLOYEE, EXPERIENCE, FAST, FIRM, FUNCTION, GAIN, HIRE, HOURS,
MAID, MEET, MOTIVATION, MOVER, NOTARY, NURSE, OCCUPATION,
OFFICE, OVERTIME, PERSONNEL, POST, PROFESSION, REPAIR,
REWARDING, ROUTINE, SALARY, SCHEDULE, SELL, SHIFT, STORES,
STRESS, TOOLS, WEEK, WORKPLACE

A Welcome Pat on the Back

Solution: 6 letters

G	I	V	E	T	E	R	A	N	S	H	M	S	P	F
S	O	S	D	N	A	B	S	U	H	N	R	A	D	E
S	K	R	E	L	C	H	U	M	S	E	S	S	E	A
T	G	O	O	D	C	O	E	P	H	T	T	L	I	T
A	F	R	O	C	H	C	U	T	O	A	G	E	R	S
P	R	I	A	C	I	W	O	R	K	E	R	S	T	R
P	I	R	G	N	L	M	S	E	A	S	T	U	G	E
R	E	W	A	R	D	I	N	G	S	G	D	N	A	H
E	N	W	S	N	R	F	A	P	S	E	I	I	T	C
C	D	A	A	F	E	I	A	B	N	M	V	N	K	A
I	S	R	A	A	N	R	L	T	O	R	I	I	G	E
A	G	M	R	I	E	E	S	C	H	S	I	L	W	T
T	E	N	N	N	S	S	L	A	P	E	S	G	E	E
E	E	G	T	S	S	E	C	C	U	S	R	E	H	S
D	H	S	I	W	W	R	I	T	E	R	S	S	S	T

APPRECIATED, BLESS, BOSSES, CARE, CHILDREN, CHUMS, CLERKS, COOKS, EARNED, ENCOURAGING, FAME, FEATS, FRIENDS, GAINING, GIFT, GIVE, GLEE, GOOD, GRANDFATHERS, GRANDMOTHERS, HAND, HUSBANDS, KIDS, NICE, PALS, PARENTS, PASTORS, POET, REWARDING, RIGHT, SMILES, STAKE, STUDENTS, SUCCESS, TEACHERS, TEAM, TEST, TRIED, VETERANS, WARM, WELCOMING, WISH, WIVES, WORKERS, WRITERS

103

About Ants

Solution: 7 letters

R	K	L	A	W	D	G	B	S	T	I	B	A	H	S
B	E	H	A	V	I	O	R	R	E	O	E	T	L	E
L	L	P	T	C	D	W	O	O	D	I	G	L	I	T
C	A	R	R	Y	I	P	W	F	U	N	C	R	O	I
R	M	A	E	O	S	P	N	M	E	N	A	E	S	H
E	C	D	E	N	D	S	O	L	T	B	D	M	P	W
K	S	S	A	R	G	U	T	R	D	O	A	M	E	S
R	C	R	S	N	T	T	C	O	T	L	P	U	E	T
O	T	A	U	H	N	S	M	T	L	S	T	S	D	R
W	A	L	L	A	I	E	L	C	I	D	E	P	I	O
F	A	E	L	B	N	P	T	D	I	O	Y	R	H	N
Y	G	P	E	Q	U	E	E	N	S	A	N	D	O	G
S	E	L	C	Y	C	N	E	C	A	S	T	E	A	F
U	E	J	O	B	S	E	R	V	A	T	I	O	N	L
B	S	G	G	E	W	I	N	G	S	P	A	R	T	R

ABDOMEN, ADAPT, ANTENNA, BEHAVIOR, BLACK, BODY, BROWN, BUSY, CARRY, CASTE, CRACK, CYCLE, DENSE, DINE, EGGS, FOOD, FOREST, GRASS, GROUND, HABITS, HIDE, HOLE, JOBS, LADY, LEAF, LEGS, LENGTH, LOTS, MALE, MOUTH, OBSERVATION, OCELLUS, PEDICLE, PEST, PLANT, QUEEN, REPRODUCTION, SAND, SMALL, SOIL, SPECIES, SPEED, SPOT, STRONG, SUMMER, TRANSPORT, TRAPS, TREE, TROPICAL, WALK, WALL, WHITE, WINGS, WOOD, WORKER

104

Albert Camus

Solution: 14 letters

E	T	D	R	A	M	A	T	X	S	T	I	W	R	L
E	O	E	U	G	A	L	P	E	A	E	M	O	O	E
S	A	T	S	E	U	G	F	I	A	O	T	I	H	B
S	S	Y	A	L	P	I	R	E	V	C	J	S	T	O
A	T	H	L	E	T	E	S	E	E	O	H	T	U	N
Y	E	T	S	N	G	R	T	R	U	L	D	E	A	J
S	C	T	S	L	W	S	I	R	T	R	I	N	R	P
R	E	A	A	I	I	D	N	E	E	E	W	N	O	I
A	E	A	L	L	L	A	D	L	U	T	R	L	G	M
N	B	F	E	I	L	A	I	R	H	X	I	A	S	F
G	O	V	O	I	G	G	R	E	E	T	T	R	R	R
E	O	C	S	R	I	U	A	O	I	A	I	E	W	A
N	K	M	E	O	M	T	L	C	M	T	N	M	L	N
I	S	A	U	S	E	E	S	A	S	C	G	S	E	K
M	T	S	U	R	A	D	R	E	H	P	Y	S	I	S

ALGERIA, ALGIERS, ATHLETE, AUTHOR, BOOKS, CALIGULA, DARU, DIRECTOR, DRAMA, DREAN, ESSAYS, FEELING, FRANK, FRENCH, GREAT, GUEST, JOURNALISM, JUSTES, MONDOVI, MORALIST, MOVE, NOBEL, NOCES, NOVELIST, PESTE, PLAGUE, PLAYS, POLITICS, RANGE, RARE, REFORMER, RELIGIOUS, RIEUX, SISYPHE, STIRS, TEACHER, THEATER, TIMES, TOAST, WILL, WITS, WRITER, WRITING

105

All about Doors

S	H	Y	P	N	E	Y	N	J	R	E	V	A	E	L
N	C	O	A	J	A	R	K	T	A	A	M	A	L	S
L	T	R	N	W	A	M	C	N	U	M	P	E	S	R
S	A	E	E	B	R	L	S	L	O	H	B	P	T	K
H	P	T	L	E	O	O	T	E	K	C	I	W	E	A
O	A	T	T	S	N	B	O	A	L	T	K	Y	P	R
G	S	L	E	I	A	B	R	D	O	A	S	S	K	T
J	S	O	L	R	C	Y	M	M	U	L	S	C	C	H
N	A	B	R	O	E	E	S	I	V	E	A	E	I	R
S	G	I	D	O	W	T	C	T	R	B	L	N	P	O
Y	E	E	L	F	O	E	U	G	E	L	G	O	C	U
R	H	C	R	S	N	M	E	O	D	E	R	A	D	G
T	O	A	R	T	U	H	S	N	O	T	L	E	O	H
N	M	P	E	E	P	H	O	L	E	L	B	U	O	D
E	E	R	D	U	T	C	H	R	S	G	N	I	W	S

ADMIT, AJAR, BACK, BARN, BARRIER, BELL, BOLT, CALL, CELL, CLOSE, CODE, DOORWAY, DOUBLE, DUTCH, EGRESS, ENTER, ENTRY, FRAME, GATEWAY, HALLOWEEN, HINGE, HOME, JAILS, JAMB, KEYS, KNOCK, LATCH, LATTICE, LEAVE, LOBBY, LOUVRED, OPEN, OUTER, PANEL, PASSAGE, PATCH, PEEPHOLE, PORTER, RAPPER, ROOMS, SALESMAN, SCREEN, SECRET, SHUT, SLAM, STEEL, STEP, STOP, STORM, SWINGS, THROUGH, TONS, VAULT, WICKET, WOOD

Aluminum

Solution: 8 letters

S	H	W	O	R	K	A	B	L	E	S	T	O	P	D
E	S	H	A	P	E	D	E	H	S	U	R	B	O	M
I	I	E	Y	B	P	N	R	O	B	O	T	O	E	U
T	N	L	N	R	I	A	I	E	P	A	R	T	T	I
R	I	G	A	K	E	K	P	A	C	K	A	G	E	R
E	F	E	N	Y	C	V	E	W	T	L	L	O	E	A
P	L	A	Q	U	E	I	L	H	L	N	L	D	H	L
O	U	R	L	I	A	R	H	I	E	R	O	T	S	O
R	S	R	W	C	R	P	C	T	S	X	Y	C	E	S
P	U	I	P	O	R	E	I	E	I	P	S	E	T	S
G	R	A	Y	O	T	F	S	D	E	I	T	F	A	M
E	F	P	D	K	S	H	E	I	G	Z	A	O	L	E
X	A	U	A	I	I	E	G	N	S	R	L	I	P	L
I	C	E	G	N	I	H	S	I	C	T	F	L	E	T
T	E	D	Y	G	S	R	E	F	L	E	C	T	O	R

ALLOY, BIKE, BRUSHED, CONTAINER, COOKING, CRAFT, DOOR, EXIT, FENCE, FINISH, FLAT, FOIL, GEAR, GRAY, HINGE, LAYER, LIGHT, METALLIC, OXIDE, PACKAGE, PANS, PART, PIECE, PLAQUE, PLATE, POTS, PRODUCT, PROPERTIES, PURPOSE, RAIL, REFLECTOR, RESIST, ROBOT, SETS, SHAPED, SHEET, SHINY, SIGNS, SILVERY, SMELT, SOLARIUM, STORE, SURFACE, THICKNESS, TUBE, TYPE, WHITE, WIRE, WORKABLE

107

An Old-Fashioned Picnic

Solution: 6 letters

P	O	P	C	O	R	N	B	D	A	S	E	H	C	S
S	W	I	N	G	C	F	S	Y	O	E	R	S	H	L
D	E	E	F	P	O	C	D	A	S	O	I	I	I	L
S	B	L	S	L	O	N	A	E	L	T	F	L	P	O
E	O	S	K	E	A	T	H	S	G	A	M	E	S	R
K	O	S	M	C	X	C	A	D	I	M	D	R	S	H
A	K	O	S	H	I	O	M	T	A	O	O	S	R	O
C	S	M	C	W	Y	P	B	S	O	T	N	O	E	L
M	O	N	D	R	I	L	U	N	C	H	E	S	Z	I
H	U	N	T	O	E	M	R	R	H	A	M	S	I	D
M	A	S	T	T	O	S	G	A	B	D	E	E	N	A
S	A	P	T	E	O	G	E	C	D	K	A	A	A	Y
P	E	U	P	A	S	T	R	E	A	I	T	E	G	L
K	C	A	P	Y	R	T	S	S	O	S	S	A	R	G
E	Z	I	R	P	T	D	S	K	R	A	P	H	O	B

BAGS, BOOKS, BOXES, BREAD, CAKES, CANDY, CHIPS, CONTESTS, DATES, FEED, FIRE, FOLKS, FOOD, GAMES, GOOD, GRASS, HAMBURGERS, HAMS, HAPPY, HOLIDAY, LETTUCE, LUNCHES, MEAL, MEATS, MOSS, MUNCH, MUSTARD, OCCASIONS, ORGANIZERS, PACK, PARKS, PASTRY, PICKLES, POPCORN, POTATO, PRIZE, RACES, RADISH, RELISH, ROAD, ROLLS, SALADS, SANDWICHES, SOME, STAND, SWIM, SWING, TOMATOES, TOTS, ZOO

Anyone for Sharks?

Solution: 11 letters

G	N	Y	R	R	A	U	Q	D	F	A	R	G	S	S
N	S	O	F	I	S	H	E	R	M	E	N	B	E	W
I	R	R	I	S	K	P	E	W	T	I	E	S	I	A
P	E	B	G	T	T	V	H	A	N	A	R	L	R	J
A	H	E	N	H	A	I	W	E	S	E	I	V	O	M
E	P	A	I	W	T	N	T	T	M	B	A	I	T	R
L	A	C	T	E	S	H	I	M	C	A	G	E	S	D
P	R	H	E	S	G	G	I	A	R	E	M	A	C
O	G	E	K	I	C	W	N	Y	A	G	I	N	B	E
W	O	S	R	C	S	R	R	I	N	M	G	S	I	V
E	N	F	A	N	A	U	O	I	T	E	I	R	T	I
R	A	A	M	T	F	T	T	R	R	H	I	E	I	S
F	E	P	R	E	D	A	T	O	R	S	G	V	N	S
U	C	T	A	L	E	S	U	A	O	E	N	I	G	A
L	O	S	R	E	T	S	N	O	M	M	T	D	S	M

ATTACK, BAIT, BEACHES, BEAST, BITINGS, CAGES, CAMERA, DANGEROUS, DEPTH, DIVERS, EATING, FISHERMEN, FRIGHTENING, FURY, IMAGINATION, JAWS, LEAPING, MARKETING, MASSIVE, MESH, MONSTERS, MOVIES, OCEANOGRAPHERS, POWERFUL, PREDATORS, QUARRY, RISK, ROLE, SIGHTINGS, STORIES, SWIMMERS, TALES, TERROR, WATER, WAVE, WHITE

109

Aromatherapy

Solution: 8 letters

D	S	W	D	E	A	E	A	T	R	E	E	S	O	S
L	N	N	L	B	M	L	D	E	L	L	F	I	S	K
C	I	A	O	Y	L	I	A	A	P	L	L	P	L	C
M	I	J	H	I	F	C	H	P	O	Y	R	A	F	I
J	O	T	N	F	T	N	A	R	G	A	R	F	L	T
J	A	A	U	I	I	O	A	N	Y	U	I	I	N	S
H	V	S	O	E	E	L	L	S	T	N	M	E	E	C
S	E	N	M	S	P	S	Y	A	S	E	M	S	R	D
R	S	R	H	I	R	A	N	R	V	T	S	E	S	N
A	C	A	B	E	N	F	R	X	A	E	A	N	M	O
J	V	A	W	T	A	E	A	E	N	M	N	A	E	P
E	S	O	N	C	Y	L	R	T	H	O	E	D	H	S
E	L	A	I	D	E	T	I	O	E	T	M	S	E	E
F	L	A	O	R	L	A	M	N	S	S	A	E	O	R
P	L	B	S	L	L	E	M	S	G	W	T	B	L	R

APPLE, BASE, BATHE, BODY, CANDLE, CREAM, DIFFUSER, ESSENTIAL, FACIAL, FLORAL, FLOWERS, FRAGRANT, HAND, HEALING, HERB, HOME, INHALE, JARS, JASMINE, JOJOBA, LAVENDER, LEMON, LIME, LOTIONS, MIND, NATURAL, OILY, PLANT, REACTIONS, RELAX, RESPOND, ROSEMARY, SENSE, SHAVE, SMELL, SNIFF, SPRAYS, STEAM, STICKS, TEST, THERAPEUTIC, THYME, TREATMENT, TREES, VANILLA, WASH

At the Dealership

Solution: 9 letters

S	E	M	K	L	K	E	L	L	A	C	E	R	N	L
R	R	R	U	O	T	C	C	S	O	H	T	O	O	B
E	A	A	U	C	T	I	O	N	T	A	S	C	I	T
P	P	L	C	K	N	V	T	T	E	R	A	N	T	R
A	M	A	E	A	R	R	T	R	S	T	A	B	A	A
I	O	R	H	A	A	E	U	L	I	E	A	P	R	V
R	C	C	E	C	S	S	L	O	S	R	G	E	A	E
S	E	H	T	T	N	E	N	C	G	N	Q	L	P	L
M	D	A	I	I	A	L	R	A	I	U	U	C	E	T
R	E	N	N	A	B	I	I	L	E	E	O	E	R	R
E	G	G	A	O	P	N	L	S	F	N	T	V	P	U
K	R	E	R	T	A	E	T	D	T	N	E	I	L	C
A	N	R	E	E	S	U	C	E	H	A	L	R	A	K
M	O	D	E	L	N	P	S	S	I	O	R	D	E	R
W	S	F	L	E	E	T	E	U	T	L	R	I	D	E

ALARM, AUCTION, BANNER, BARGAIN, BOOTH, BORROW, CARS, CHANGE, CHARTER, CLERK, COMPARE, CONTEST, CONTRACT, DEAL, DRIVE, FLEET, INSURE, LEASE, LINEUP, LOAN, LOCAL, LOCATION, LOCK, MAKE, MECHANIC, MODEL, ORDER, PARK, PARTS, PILOT, PREPARATION, QUOTE, RECALL, RENT, REPAIRS, REQUEST, RETAIL, RIDE, SCRIPTED, SELLING, SERVICE, STANDS, STOCK, TESTING, TOUR, TRAVEL, TRUCK, USED, VALUE, VANS

111

Back to School

Solution: 10 letters

S	H	A	L	L	S	T	W	T	X	E	T	S	T	G
S	K	O	A	A	H	A	C	R	N	S	R	S	R	V
S	E	O	M	E	T	E	Y	I	I	E	E	A	I	A
A	G	H	O	E	J	E	T	D	E	T	D	S	D	P
S	T	R	C	B	W	E	I	P	U	U	I	U	E	Y
K	Y	T	U	N	A	O	S	S	A	T	L	N	T	E
I	O	S	E	C	U	F	R	T	S	T	S	L	G	S
L	G	O	H	N	U	L	E	K	S	A	U	E	R	S
L	N	E	B	T	D	N	V	D	S	C	L	E	U	S
S	R	E	U	R	R	A	I	D	A	L	K	C	E	T
S	L	R	O	A	A	P	N	F	O	C	C	D	C	P
L	E	O	E	P	L	E	U	C	O	E	A	A	R	A
I	M	L	P	O	I	M	Y	L	E	R	X	O	P	S
A	E	L	M	R	E	A	D	D	G	E	M	A	N	S
F	Y	A	F	E	T	E	P	M	O	C	R	A	M	T

ADULTS, APPLY, ATTENDANCE, BELL, BOOKS, CAPS, CLASS, COLLEGE, COMPETE, CRAM, DIPLOMA, EXACT, EXAM, FACULTY, FAIL, FRIENDS, FUTURE, GOAL, GRADES, GRADUATE, HALLS, HOMEWORK, LATE, LEARN, LOCKERS, LUNCHES, PASS, PEERS, PENS, PROM, READ, ROOM, SKILLS, STUDENT, STUDY, SUBJECT, SUCCEED, TEACHERS, TEST, TEXT, THEORY, UNIVERSITY, VISIT, WRITING, YEARBOOK

112

Batteries Not Included

Solution: 7 letters

W	D	D	I	C	A	E	R	I	N	S	E	R	T	R
E	E	A	M	L	Y	E	S	S	E	L	D	R	O	C
M	S	K	L	A	G	L	L	E	C	W	A	T	C	H
A	U	O	C	R	N	N	I	D	N	Z	P	S	L	S
G	Y	I	A	A	I	U	E	N	O	A	T	K	T	M
D	F	H	H	C	P	G	F	R	D	R	G	R	L	H
I	C	L	K	T	R	P	A	A	U	R	E	N	E	O
A	S	E	A	A	I	L	L	C	C	W	I	A	A	H
G	L	L	H	S	O	L	K	I	O	T	D	C	K	M
N	O	C	O	S	H	P	A	P	A	P	U	U	A	T
I	E	I	D	O	L	L	E	H	N	P	R	B	L
R	S	I	D	E	T	A	I	O	Z	R	C	R	E	O
A	R	E	M	A	C	C	N	G	I	I	A	E	M	V
E	A	S	T	O	R	E	E	C	H	N	S	N	S	A
H	C	T	O	Y	S	D	E	N	D	T	S	T	E	S

ACID, ADAPTOR, ALKALINE, ALLOY, APPLIANCES, BRAND, CAMERA, CARS, CELL, CHARGER, CORDLESS, CURRENT, CYLINDRICAL, DOLL, FLASHLIGHT, GAME, HEADPHONES, HEARING AID, HERTZ, INSERT, LAST, LEAK, LITHIUM, MANGANESE, MANUFACTURE, NICKEL, OHMS, PACK, PLACED, POWER, PRICE, RADIO, RAZOR, RECHARGED, SETS, SIDE, SIZE, SOLAR, STORE, TOOLS, TOYS, TRUCK, USED, VOLT, WATCH

113

Beans

E	P	O	D	S	T	A	B	U	S	H	E	L	L	S
I	L	I	H	C	N	E	Y	E	L	L	O	W	J	O
S	E	B	E	N	A	M	L	O	B	O	A	A	Z	U
T	A	V	A	F	L	O	U	R	S	X	C	N	J	P
R	N	E	L	T	P	S	O	S	E	K	A	U	A	T
I	B	W	T	E	E	A	G	D	H	B	R	N	S	E
N	A	O	H	V	D	G	L	N	R	Y	S	O	L	T
G	S	E	Y	I	E	D	E	A	I	E	P	B	P	N
S	N	V	P	C	T	A	G	V	A	N	I	L	L	A
H	A	S	O	W	S	E	U	E	N	D	I	E	I	I
N	C	E	S	R	O	H	M	L	E	I	C	W	S	D
P	A	T	J	U	I	C	E	V	E	K	R	U	T	N
A	L	M	E	U	H	C	N	E	R	F	O	A	R	I
S	E	N	I	V	M	L	I	T	G	Y	P	O	E	D
S	T	A	P	L	E	P	L	E	E	F	F	O	C	Y

BEAN, BROAD, BUSH, CANS, CHILI, CIVET, COFFEE, COOK, COWPEA, CROP, CURD, EDIBLE, EGGS, FAVA, FRENCH, GARBANZO, GREEN, HEAD, HEALTHY, HORSE, INDIAN, JACK, JUICE, JUMP, KIDNEY, LEAN, LEGUME, LIMA, LINE, LIST, LOCUST, MUSHY, NAVY, PASS, PLANT, PODS, POLES, PORK, POST, SHELLS, SNAP, SOME, SOUP, SOWS, SOYA, STAPLE, STRINGS, TOSS, TWINING, VANILLA, VEGETABLE, VELVET, VETCH, VINES, WAXED, WHITE, YEAR, YELLOW

Beethoven

Solution: 10 letters

G	C	L	A	S	S	I	C	A	L	H	T	X	I	S
I	H	H	T	N	I	N	L	A	R	O	T	S	A	P
W	T	N	A	V	A	M	N	O	I	L	E	D	I	F
D	U	D	I	M	I	O	R	O	A	R	E	P	O	S
U	R	D	R	S	I	E	S	S	B	N	E	N	N	Y
L	T	E	S	I	P	X	T	O	O	L	A	O	N	M
A	G	A	S	M	H	I	L	I	U	I	I	M	I	P
R	S	F	E	O	N	T	T	R	P	T	F	U	L	H
T	A	N	V	G	P	I	O	P	I	S	R	S	O	O
S	T	E	I	L	D	M	E	S	A	O	E	I	I	N
E	A	S	F	A	A	R	O	U	N	L	E	C	V	I
H	N	S	R	N	I	P	A	C	I	O	R	E	M	E
C	O	T	T	O	M	I	N	A	S	W	O	R	K	S
R	S	I	D	O	T	S	T	E	T	R	A	U	Q	I
O	C	S	C	O	N	C	E	R	T	O	A	N	E	J

BONN, CLASSICAL, COMPOSER, COMPOSITIONS, CONCERTO, DEAFNESS, EMPEROR, EROICA, FIDELIO, FIVE, FREE, GERMAN, JENA, LASTING, LUDWIG, MISSA, MIX, MUSIC, NINTH, OPERA, ORCHESTRAL, PASTORAL, PERIODS, PIANIST, PIANO, QUARTETS, ROMANTIC, RULE, SIXTH, SOLO, SONATAS, SYMPHONIES, THIRD, TRADITION, TRUTH, VAN, VIOLIN, VIRTUOSO, WORKS

115

Bell Peppers

E	N	I	V	R	Y	C	G	D	D	L	W	P	A	D
R	N	I	I	E	H	T	E	S	U	E	L	A	E	S
H	S	N	R	I	V	T	S	F	E	E	V	F	L	S
S	G	U	N	A	A	I	R	I	N	C	F	L	T	S
S	A	E	O	N	L	O	T	T	E	U	U	E	A	S
T	S	L	I	I	V	U	I	A	T	F	W	A	G	H
E	I	R	A	A	C	F	P	S	R	S	E	O	S	A
M	A	F	L	D	U	I	B	O	C	O	O	K	E	D
M	A	F	N	L	S	C	L	R	P	D	C	U	A	E
D	R	R	E	O	H	O	O	E	I	E	U	E	P	B
F	E	I	K	O	C	S	S	A	D	B	I	P	D	S
R	L	C	P	E	E	A	S	Z	I	R	S	A	S	W
I	E	P	I	E	T	L	O	Z	C	E	I	H	D	O
E	E	A	D	P	N	S	M	I	E	H	N	S	E	R
D	P	S	L	S	S	A	S	P	D	N	E	E	R	G

BAKE, BLOSSOMS, CHINESE, CHOPPED, COLORFUL, CONFIT, COOKED, CUISINE, DECORATIVE, DELICIOUS, DICED, FEISTY, FLAVORFUL, FRIED, GOOD, GREEN, GROW, HALVED, HERBED, MARINATED, MARKETS, PEEL, PIZZA, PLENTIFUL, POPULAR, REAL, REDS, RIBS, RINGS, RIPEN, SALADS, SALSA, SAUCES, SEEDS, SHADE, SHAPE, SLAW, SOUPS, SPICED, STEWS, STUFFED, VINE

Brahms

Solution: 11 letters

O	L	O	S	N	N	A	M	U	H	C	S	I	W	N
R	C	S	C	N	T	A	L	E	N	T	N	R	O	D
E	H	I	E	O	O	S	I	C	O	S	S	E	L	Y
S	O	A	T	I	N	I	T	C	T	P	O	Q	F	A
J	Y	R	I	N	H	D	T	R	I	O	E	U	E	H
S	O	M	C	L	A	P	U	I	U	S	N	I	N	C
T	N	H	P	H	G	M	A	C	S	C	U	E	O	D
G	U	O	A	H	E	A	O	R	T	O	T	M	S	O
R	F	T	I	N	O	S	C	R	G	O	P	U	D	O
U	E	A	T	T	N	N	T	A	V	O	R	M	R	G
B	E	A	M	I	A	E	I	R	S	I	I	G	O	E
M	L	R	T	E	M	I	S	E	A	S	E	B	H	C
A	E	D	U	A	R	D	R	O	S	L	A	N	C	A
H	I	R	E	D	E	I	L	A	L	R	E	P	N	P
O	N	A	I	P	G	S	T	A	V	C	L	A	R	A

ALLEGRO, BIOGRAPHIES, CHORDS, CLARA, COMPOSER, COMPOSITIONS, CONDUCTOR, COSSEL, EDUARD, FAME, FEEL, FLOW, GERMAN, GOOD, HAIL, HAMBURG, HAYDN, INSTRUMENTAL, JOHANNES, LIEDER, MERIT, MUSICIAN, ORCHESTRAL, PACE, PASSACAGLIA, PIANO, REQUIEM, ROMANTIC, SCHUMANN, SOLO, SOUND, STRUCTURE, SYMPHONIES, TALENT, TONES, TUNE, TUTTI, VARIATIONS, VIENNA

117

Breathe Easy

Solution: 7 letters

N	C	E	L	L	S	N	P	E	T	A	M	I	N	A
T	I	S	S	U	E	S	G	M	E	L	A	H	N	I
W	R	B	S	P	A	G	E	N	U	T	T	T	W	R
H	C	A	O	G	U	R	E	C	I	P	L	U	O	W
I	U	T	C	L	N	R	A	N	O	S	E	O	L	A
S	L	M	P	T	G	U	E	T	A	R	X	M	B	Y
T	A	O	F	Y	F	O	L	E	U	Y	P	I	P	E
L	T	S	E	F	I	L	M	S	G	V	I	T	A	L
E	E	P	U	V	U	D	H	E	W	A	F	T	T	O
T	C	H	H	S	L	P	N	V	H	L	S	R	E	D
S	C	E	N	T	N	A	P	A	E	V	A	S	N	O
E	I	R	E	S	T	O	S	E	P	E	A	I	A	R
H	L	E	V	E	N	I	R	H	H	X	W	N	E	P
C	I	C	O	U	G	H	L	E	P	X	E	U	L	B
X	A	R	O	H	T	E	A	S	E	L	C	S	U	M

AIRWAY, ALVEOLI, ANIMATE, ATMOSPHERE, BLOW, BLUE, CELLS, CHEST, CILIA, CIRCULATE, COUGH, EASE, ENERGY, EVEN, EXPAND, EXPEL, GASP, GULP, HEART, HEAVE, HEMOGLOBIN, HUFF, INHALE, LEAN, LIFE, LOBE, LUNGS, MOUTH, MUSCLES, NOSE, ODOR, OPEN, OXYGENATE, PANT, PASSAGE, PIPE, PROCESS, PUFF, PUMP, RATE, REST, RUSH, SAVE, SCENT, SIGH, SING, SINUS, SNORE, THORAX, TISSUES, TRACT, TUNE, VALVE, VITAL, WAFT, WHISTLE, WIND

Bursaries

Solution: 10 letters

C	R	O	E	D	S	S	E	S	T	E	E	V	A	S
N	U	D	C	I	E	N	E	N	T	R	A	T	E	D
E	L	L	I	W	I	S	A	M	S	U	H	R	G	R
M	I	E	O	F	T	W	E	E	E	L	D	N	N	A
E	N	C	H	U	I	T	S	R	E	S	I	I	P	W
D	G	N	C	N	N	R	S	T	V	T	T	P	E	A
A	L	E	N	D	U	I	E	T	I	I	L	E	M	S
C	A	I	L	O	T	S	V	R	U	I	N	E	R	R
A	N	C	C	L	R	P	W	E	C	D	D	G	E	S
G	G	S	D	I	O	S	H	A	R	I	E	S	I	E
G	U	R	O	E	P	C	T	Y	C	S	E	N	E	S
R	A	W	A	O	P	I	O	I	S	A	I	R	T	H
E	G	I	R	N	O	L	N	S	R	I	G	T	T	S
A	E	T	N	N	T	E	E	C	T	E	C	A	Y	I
T	S	S	S	S	N	S	H	H	D	S	M	S	S	W

ACADEME, APPLICATIONS, ATHLETES, AWARDS, CHOICE, COLLEGE, COSTS, COURSES, DEGREE, DESERVING, EARN, FINE, FUND, GAINS, GRANTS, GREAT, HELPED, LANGUAGES, MATH, MEDICINE, OPPORTUNITIES, PHYSICS, RATED, RESEARCH, RULING, SAVE, SCIENCE, SEMESTERS, SIGN, SPORTS, STUDENTS, STUDIES, UNIVERSITY, WANT, WILL, WINNING, WISH, WITS, WRITING

119

Business Cards

Solution: 5 letters

S	E	L	F	E	M	P	L	O	Y	E	D	E	E	N
Y	A	L	P	S	I	D	G	S	N	T	A	K	E	E
L	C	M	H	C	H	I	S	A	L	E	S	P	R	G
L	O	G	O	P	R	O	M	O	T	E	E	A	G	N
A	W	L	N	L	L	E	W	G	F	S	M	R	E	A
C	O	A	E	G	P	U	N	S	A	F	A	T	D	H
R	R	T	L	T	E	I	N	C	S	L	I	Y	I	C
Y	K	F	N	L	R	L	D	C	U	O	L	C	R	X
N	E	I	A	B	E	S	T	L	H	T	B	C	E	E
A	R	H	G	I	F	T	L	I	N	M	O	H	C	R
P	S	S	O	K	S	E	D	E	T	O	O	D	T	U
M	E	L	L	C	L	G	N	L	U	K	O	O	T	C
O	L	O	S	V	D	A	E	T	R	N	I	O	R	C
C	L	O	E	V	E	E	L	S	M	I	N	G	L	E
R	O	T	A	N	I	D	R	O	O	C	G	O	A	L

AGENT, BEST, BOOKING, BOSS, BRING, CALL, CASE, CELLULAR, CLIENTS, COLOR, COMPANY, COOL, COORDINATOR, COWORKERS, DEAL, DEGREE, DESK, DIPLOMAS, DIRECTOR, DISPLAY, EMAIL, EXCHANGE, GIFT, GLOSSY, GOAL, GOOD, HOLDER, HOURS, LECTURE, LOGO, LUNCH, MINGLE, NAME, NEED, OFFICE, PARTY, PHONE, PRINT, PROMOTE, ROOM, SALES, SELF EMPLOYED, SELL, SHIFT, SHOWS, SLEEVE, SLOGAN, TAKE, TITLE, TOOL, WALLET

Candles

Solution: 7 letters

W	F	T	T	S	L	F	E	Y	L	H	C	R	O	T
I	I	T	E	F	R	T	R	C	T	A	E	R	T	A
N	I	S	A	A	I	H	O	A	N	E	R	M	R	R
D	A	N	H	P	L	G	O	T	G	A	I	O	O	T
G	W	C	C	E	E	I	M	A	I	R	M	R	L	H
D	E	O	E	E	R	R	G	E	R	A	A	O	A	F
L	N	T	L	S	N	B	S	H	T	E	I	N	R	V
M	E	O	A	B	U	S	A	H	T	G	D	E	C	S
S	S	O	M	R	I	O	E	L	N	M	L	L	K	E
S	O	I	N	L	O	R	H	I	A	A	O	C	O	C
A	R	I	T	R	A	C	T	D	X	R	I	O	S	H
L	N	A	A	P	R	E	E	H	O	W	O	E	D	E
G	L	N	Y	U	A	U	K	D	D	I	X	L	L	K
L	G	E	H	T	A	B	O	E	M	A	L	F	O	A
E	T	C	E	L	L	O	C	P	W	R	Y	S	M	C

ALMOND, AROMATHERAPY, BAPTISM, BATH, BIRTHDAY, BLOW,
BRIGHT, BURNING, CAKE, CHAR, CHURCH, COLLECT, COLOR,
DECORATE, FLAME, FLORAL, FRAGRANCE, GASES, GIFT, GLASS,
HANDMADE, HEAT, HERBAL, HOLDER, HOME, HOUSE, IGNITE,
INCENSE, MOLD, MOOD, NOEL, OILS, ORANGE, POUR, RELAX,
ROMANCE, ROOM, ROSE, TALL, TAPERS, TART, TEA LIGHT, TORCH,
TREAT, VARIETY, WAXES, WICKS, WIND, WISH

121

Candy Canes

Solution: 9 letters

S	Y	T	E	I	R	A	V	C	W	E	H	C	E
R	P	R	C	R	S	A	T	N	A	S	P	P	P
I	C	E	L	E	B	R	A	T	I	O	N	A	A
B	O	E	A	G	R	E	E	N	K	C	O	R	N
B	L	S	S	R	T	S	R	E	T	U	Y	W	D
O	O	B	S	F	M	A	T	H	O	L	D	T	P
N	R	A	I	I	G	I	B	R	L	G	E	E	S
I	S	G	C	T	H	S	N	O	I	E	P	M	T
M	E	S	A	W	E	P	J	T	W	P	R	R	N
A	N	S	R	I	A	Y	T	S	E	S	E	T	E
G	T	E	D	S	M	K	K	R	E	S	T	S	M
E	N	V	S	T	O	C	M	A	S	Z	N	O	A
L	A	L	S	O	I	I	R	E	D	S	I	C	N
A	I	E	H	L	N	T	D	R	A	H	W	S	R
S	G	A	T	T	S	S	E	M	S	Y	M	B	O

BAGS, BITE, BOWS, BOXES, CARDS, CELEBRATION, CHEW, CLASSIC, COLORS, COST, DESSERT, ELVES, GARNISH, GIANT, GIFT, GLUCOSE, GREEN, HAND, HARD, HOLD, HOOK, IMAGE, JOLLY, LICK, MELT, MESS, ORNAMENTS, PANS, PASS, PEPPERMINT, REDS, RIBBON, ROCK, SALE, SANTA, SEASON, SENT, SHAPE, SIZE, SPEARMINT, STICKY, STRIPES, SWEET, SYMBOL, SYRUP, TAGS, TREE, TWIST, VARIETY, WHITE, WINTER, WRAP

Caught in Traffic

Solution: 8 letters

S	R	A	L	U	L	L	E	C	S	P	C	H	D	C
D	N	A	L	S	I	B	R	T	O	E	O	A	L	P
L	E	G	S	N	S	O	O	L	A	U	N	O	R	A
N	F	T	I	I	S	W	I	R	R	G	S	I	L	S
O	E	A	O	S	T	C	E	S	E	U	T	M	L	S
I	R	W	I	U	E	T	C	R	R	D	R	B	T	E
T	N	N	S	L	R	A	I	E	V	O	U	U	I	N
S	G	D	A	P	U	E	K	N	T	E	C	M	M	G
E	I	T	I	G	A	R	P	S	G	K	T	P	E	E
G	E	G	H	V	A	P	E	A	W	R	I	E	N	R
N	X	T	N	P	I	R	E	N	I	O	O	R	R	M
O	I	E	H	A	V	D	O	R	T	R	N	U	U	I
C	T	O	G	I	L	G	U	A	R	E	S	S	T	L
I	N	E	C	A	P	S	Y	A	D	D	R	L	E	E
E	R	E	P	O	R	T	H	A	L	T	O	C	R	K

BORED, BUMPER, CARS, CAUGHT, CELLULAR, CLOSURE, CONGESTION, CONSTRUCTION, CROSSING, DANGER, DAYS, DETOUR, ENTER, EXIT, FAILURE, GATE, HALT, HOURS, INDIVIDUAL, ISLAND, LATE, LEGS, LINES, MILE, NEWSPAPER, PARK, PASSENGER, PHONE, POLICE, POOLS, RAGE, REPAIRS, REPORT, RETURN, ROAD, ROUTE, SERVICE, SIGNAL, SIGNS, SITTING, SNOW, SPACE, STORM, STUCK, SWERVE, TIME, TRAIN

123

Cell Phones

Solution: 4 letters

S	B	U	S	Y	E	K	E	Y	R	E	T	T	A	B
S	T	T	E	M	T	V	D	P	A	I	N	P	U	T
N	E	A	A	R	A	I	R	L	H	L	L	T	Y	A
R	O	I	T	W	U	O	L	E	E	A	P	C	E	N
E	L	I	R	I	M	T	A	I	N	H	N	S	O	R
W	T	I	T	O	C	D	A	G	B	E	D	I	I	E
O	A	A	T	A	S	K	I	I	G	O	T	N	G	D
P	Y	I	B	E	C	S	W	R	N	P	M	R	A	E
D	O	S	T	E	E	I	E	D	E	I	A	R	R	H
N	I	E	A	R	R	M	N	C	N	H	M	U	E	L
F	N	A	V	E	E	E	E	U	C	U	T	E	H	T
D	R	I	L	M	K	R	T	O	M	A	M	E	N	R
N	C	E	A	E	I	L	I	E	M	L	B	E	U	
E	S	O	E	N	S	O	E	F	M	L	O	L	E	K
S	R	W	G	D	R	A	C	P	O	E	Y	C	S	R

ACCESSORIES, AIRWAVE, BATTERY, BUSY, CALLS, CARD, CHARGE, COLOR, COMMUNICATION, DIAL, DISPLAY, EASY, EMAIL, EMERGENCY, ENTER, FEATURE, FREE, HANDHELD, HEADSET, HELLO, INPUT, KEEP, KEYS, MENU, MINIATURE, MINUTES, MOBILITY, NUMBER, POWER, PROMOTION, REBATE, RECEPTION, RELY, RING, ROAM, SEND, SERVICE, SIGNAL, STATIC, TASK, TEND, TERM, TIME, WEEKEND, WIRELESS

Checking into a Resort

Solution: 11 letters

G	U	E	S	T	S	R	S	S	E	G	R	A	H	C
S	O	E	S	B	S	E	W	S	N	E	E	R	G	T
S	L	U	U	O	H	I	E	S	I	N	N	E	T	N
A	K	L	R	C	M	E	L	C	S	D	R	V	A	E
T	C	I	A	M	G	O	L	F	I	N	G	M	B	M
M	O	E	I	H	E	N	R	N	U	S	B	A	L	N
O	B	N	M	N	T	T	I	P	C	I	U	S	E	I
S	G	E	I	A	G	N	S	H	E	I	U	M	S	A
P	D	S	D	C	G	T	D	N	T	O	S	T	K	T
H	O	O	P	R	R	R	C	S	I	Y	E	E	N	R
E	O	R	O	U	O	E	P	R	L	F	R	E	I	E
R	R	O	O	O	C	O	U	I	F	A	V	E	L	T
E	M	C	L	O	R	X	M	U	F	A	I	I	V	N
S	E	E	S	T	U	A	B	S	R	I	C	H	E	E
N	N	D	S	L	F	E	R	U	S	A	E	L	P	W

AMBIENCE, ATMOSPHERE, BEACHES, BEDROOMS, BUFFETS, CHARGES, CLUBS, COURTS, CUISINE, CUPS, DECOR, DINING ROOMS, DOORMEN, DROOL, ENTERTAINMENT, EVERYTHING, FAMILY, FARE, GAME, GOLFING, GOURMETS, GREENS, GUESTS, HALLS, LINKS, LUXURIOUS, MUSIC, PLEASURE, POOLS, PROMOS, RAVE, RICH, ROSE, SERVICE, SKIING, SPORTS, SWELL, SWIMMING, TABLES, TENNIS, TONIC, VIEW

125

Chewing on Artichokes

Solution: 11 letters

C	M	E	H	U	N	F	E	H	C	D	S	E	S	U
B	S	E	C	S	F	A	E	L	A	T	D	S	M	C
U	R	M	D	I	E	A	L	E	U	E	E	L	A	O
T	E	T	E	I	R	R	R	F	T	N	H	L	L	O
T	T	Y	L	T	T	P	F	A	I	Y	I	E	C	K
E	N	L	B	A	S	E	N	N	T	F	T	T	A	E
R	E	K	A	E	D	I	R	D	O	E	M	T	M	D
G	C	C	D	M	R	O	L	R	E	R	K	E	U	U
N	N	I	I	A	H	O	N	I	A	U	A	R	V	N
I	W	R	M	T	C	I	R	F	S	N	Q	G	A	E
P	O	P	R	H	A	O	G	R	S	A	E	I	T	M
P	R	O	O	T	V	L	E	E	R	U	T	A	N	P
I	G	K	F	A	O	Y	D	A	L	A	S	N	N	U
D	E	E	L	B	A	T	E	G	E	V	I	I	O	O
S	N	F	E	L	D	O	O	G	L	E	A	V	E	S

BUTTER, CALIFORNIA, CENTERS, CHEF, CHOKES, CLAMS, COLD, COOKED, DIPPING, FARM, FLAN, FLAVOR, FORMIDABLE, FRESH, GLOBE, GOOD, GROWN, HEAD, HEART, LAYERS, LEAF, LEAVES, MARINATED, MARKET, MEANS, MEAT, MEDITERRANEAN, MENU, NATURE, NUTTY, PRICE, PRICKLY, ROOT, SALAD, SOUP, STEMS, STUFFED, THORNINESS, UNIQUE, USES, VEGETABLE, VINAIGRETTE, WIDESPREAD

Choo-Choo Trains

B	U	L	K	T	R	C	S	Y	A	S	L	I	A	R
C	C	B	E	R	T	H	R	L	N	E	P	I	R	T
A	R	R	I	V	A	L	A	O	N	A	I	E	N	R
R	E	R	A	F	A	N	B	N	S	D	P	A	E	I
R	W	L	Y	T	I	R	U	C	E	S	R	M	N	D
I	V	I	O	M	N	T	T	S	P	U	O	T	O	E
E	D	N	R	P	C	I	T	Y	A	O	E	V	S	C
R	M	E	A	L	E	I	E	T	R	R	T	L	E	M
Y	T	T	P	S	N	R	S	L	S	E	A	S	R	R
A	O	H	T	A	T	E	A	E	U	O	N	A	V	C
L	C	G	T	A	R	E	C	T	C	D	K	E	I	L
E	N	I	G	N	E	T	A	R	E	L	E	C	C	A
D	O	E	R	W	I	S	U	M	S	D	T	H	E	S
N	R	R	N	O	G	A	W	R	L	O	N	G	C	S
E	B	F	N	T	N	R	S	T	E	K	C	I	T	S

ACCELERATE, ARRIVAL, BARS, BERTH, BRONCO, BULK, CARRIER, CITY, CLASS, COAL, COMPANY, CREW, CROSSOVER, DELAY, DEPARTURE, DESTINATION, ENGINE, FARE, FREIGHT, INTERSECTION, IRON, LINE, LONG, MEAL, OPERATED, RAILS, RESTAURANT, RIDE, SCENERY, SCHEDULE, SEAT, SECURITY, SERVICE, SPEED, STEAM, STOP, TANK, TERMINAL, TICKETS, TOWN, TRAVEL, TRIP, TUNNEL, VALVE, WAGON

127

Cocktail Party Talk

Solution: 11 letters

Q	U	I	P	S	B	D	U	L	L	Y	N	N	U	F
S	U	C	O	F	R	I	V	O	L	O	U	S	G	C
G	I	E	D	A	I	S	T	K	I	L	S	N	L	I
N	M	N	A	S	G	M	L	T	N	A	I	E	U	T
I	P	J	T	T	H	A	A	K	F	R	V	R	E	L
L	O	O	E	E	T	S	N	E	O	E	O	I	H	Y
K	L	Y	M	A	R	O	T	B	R	I	U	M	T	S
R	I	E	I	E	W	E	Y	E	M	Q	D	T	U	C
A	T	D	V	L	V	L	S	L	A	S	I	R	S	H
P	E	N	E	O	D	U	A	T	T	W	A	I	E	A
S	O	D	I	N	M	C	K	I	I	A	T	V	R	T
C	G	C	E	A	O	N	L	E	V	N	S	I	I	T
E	E	I	G	V	S	T	A	L	E	T	G	A	O	E
S	R	I	R	R	E	L	E	V	A	N	T	L	U	R
F	L	O	U	D	L	Y	B	U	S	I	N	E	S	S

AMUSE, BORING, BRIGHT, BUSINESS, CHATTER, CLEVER, CONVERSATION, DATE, DULL, ENJOYED, FAST, FOCUS, FRIENDLY, FRIVOLOUS, FUNNY, HUMOR, IMPOLITE, INFORMATIVE, INTERESTING, IRRELEVANT, KEEN, KNOWLEDGE, LOUDLY, QUIET, QUIPS, SAFE, SERIOUS, SHRILL, SPARKLING, STAID, STALE, STILTED, TALK, TRIVIAL, VIM, VOCAL, VOICES, WANT, WITTY

Coming to Brazil

Solution: 8 letters

E	T	H	C	A	E	B	B	A	R	B	E	C	U	E
Y	R	T	N	U	O	C	S	L	A	E	R	S	C	A
C	O	U	S	W	S	R	R	O	C	B	O	A	T	S
O	P	O	T	A	O	S	Y	N	C	I	T	M	N	E
R	I	S	G	L	V	T	A	N	Z	C	E	B	T	E
C	C	R	O	I	U	D	R	U	M	S	E	A	T	F
O	A	C	O	A	J	C	B	T	G	U	M	R	O	F
V	L	L	E	O	E	A	I	S	I	I	S	O	U	O
A	A	B	B	C	H	P	K	R	L	T	D	I	R	C
D	T	I	S	I	V	O	I	C	G	R	P	P	C	L
O	M	R	A	T	C	E	N	G	U	A	R	A	N	A
A	P	D	W	O	I	I	I	F	R	V	V	N	P	U
L	I	S	A	X	T	R	L	R	I	E	A	E	E	S
U	R	S	R	E	Y	A	O	E	L	L	S	M	L	A
L	T	I	M	E	G	T	W	N	I	A	R	A	E	C

AGRICULTURE, BAHIA, BARBECUE, BEACH, BEAUTY, BIKINI, BIRDS, BOATS, BUZIOS, CAPOEIRA, CASUAL, CITY, CLIMATE, COAST, COFFEE, COLORS, CORCOVADO, COUNTRY, DANCE, DRUMS, EXOTIC, FLAG, FOOD, GUARANA, IGUASSU, IPANEMA, JOBIM, LULA, MEET, MUSIC, NUTS, PARROT, PELE, RAIN, REAL, SAMBA, SERGIPE, SOCCER, SOUTH, TIME, TOUR, TOWN, TRAVEL, TRIP, TROPICAL, VARGAS, VAST, VIEW, VIOLA, VISIT, WARM

129

Consult the Almanac

Solution: 8 letters

F	L	S	C	A	F	Y	L	S	C	P	N	S	M	S
S	O	E	N	E	W	S	M	I	T	O	R	E	O	T
K	G	R	I	O	E	H	F	O	I	R	N	I	O	S
O	S	L	E	C	W	I	N	T	N	C	A	K	N	E
O	E	V	T	C	T	P	A	G	S	O	C	S	S	T
B	O	I	O	N	A	M	D	T	I	U	R	A	I	N
L	O	D	E	G	R	S	A	S	L	S	E	T	O	N
N	E	I	E	O	E	T	T	A	E	E	L	I	S	T
S	C	N	F	S	I	C	I	S	S	E	T	A	D	A
S	D	N	I	S	I	T	P	N	F	A	C	T	S	E
A	I	V	T	D	S	I	E	W	G	A	B	N	D	T
F	D	I	E	E	L	D	E	I	R	K	R	A	I	F
A	C	R	L	C	N	D	V	D	O	E	C	M	R	I
S	P	E	E	O	I	A	A	E	W	E	E	E	E	G
T	C	R	C	T	N	A	L	P	D	W	D	A	E	R

ADVISES, AGENDA, ARTS, ASTRONOMY, BELIEF, BOOKS, CELESTIAL, CODES, CONDENSE, CROP, DATES, DECADE, EASE, ECLIPSES, FACTS, FARMER, FAST, FORECAST, GIFT, GRAB, GROW, INFORMATION, LIST, LOGS, LOVE, LUCK, MOON, NAME, NAVIGATION, NEWS, NOTES, PLANT, PREDICTS, PRINT, RAIN, READ, SCIENTIFIC, SECTION, SHIP, SIGN, SKIES, SNOW, STATISTICS, TESTS, TIDE, TIME, WEEK, WIDE

130

Cookie Cutters

Solution: 10 letters

S	D	E	R	Y	M	N	R	S	E	L	S	O	S	Y
D	A	N	Y	L	R	E	S	T	L	E	E	R	L	N
A	E	A	U	S	O	R	A	U	V	A	E	M	S	I
F	R	T	T	O	F	D	E	L	G	T	M	T	O	T
T	B	A	A	D	R	L	E	B	S	A	N	I	H	N
B	R	E	O	R	C	I	F	U	W	A	R	G	N	S
S	E	U	G	R	O	H	L	E	H	A	I	Y	D	A
G	G	A	I	R	S	C	N	P	S	L	R	N	I	N
H	N	C	R	H	A	I	E	P	E	T	O	T	S	R
E	I	I	A	S	H	L	B	D	A	M	I	E	S	A
Z	G	P	S	T	E	E	L	U	A	R	I	V	D	B
I	E	G	N	U	R	I	A	I	T	N	T	E	E	B
S	G	U	L	R	M	I	D	R	N	T	K	I	G	I
E	T	B	Y	E	P	A	M	U	T	A	E	I	E	T
S	R	E	W	O	L	F	B	S	B	S	V	R	N	S

AMUSING, ANIMALS, BAKED, BEARS, BLUE, BUNNIES, BUTTER, CHILDREN, CIRCLE, CLUSTERS, DATE, DECORATED, DELIGHT, DIAMONDS, DOUGH, EGGS, ELEPHANTS, ELVES, FADS, FESTIVE, FLOWERS, FORM, GINGERBREAD, HEARTS, LARGE, LEMON, LIME, NUTS, PARTIES, RABBITS, RASPBERRY, REDS, ROUND, SHAPES, SIZE, STARS, STRAWBERRY, SUGARY, THIN, TINY, TRAY, TRIMS, VANILLA

131

Corporate Designs

Y	I	M	L	T	S	O	I	D	U	A	B	T	D	S
E	N	A	O	R	A	D	T	E	N	U	N	T	E	I
F	E	A	O	R	E	E	S	S	A	Y	L	C	A	A
D	I	L	P	N	A	I	R	I	I	R	C	E	I	D
T	O	E	T	M	T	L	N	G	E	I	O	M	V	V
C	N	I	G	R	O	E	E	N	H	P	A	A	R	E
C	T	E	E	A	S	C	O	E	E	G	C	N	E	R
Y	O	P	T	S	N	I	V	R	E	L	Y	T	S	T
S	X	R	P	S	T	G	A	S	P	E	C	T	S	I
E	S	S	P	A	I	T	I	W	E	L	O	G	O	S
G	R	E	T	O	I	S	S	A	U	O	A	T	E	E
N	O	S	P	O	R	N	N	I	H	R	L	O	R	M
A	B	A	N	A	R	A	T	O	G	O	D	A	K	E
H	A	S	L	I	H	E	T	O	C	N	W	S	V	N
C	L	A	S	S	N	S	S	E	T	A	S	T	E	T

ADVERTISEMENT, ASPECTS, AUDIO, AWARDS, AWARE, BUSINESS, CHANGES, CLASS, COLORS, COMPANY, CONSISTENT, CORPORATE, DEAL, DESIGNERS, EXPERTISE, GIANT, GOALS, GREAT, IDENTITY, IMAGE, LABOR, LOGOS, LOOK, MORALE, NAME, OPERATIONS, PAINT, SERVICE, SHAPES, SHOW, SIGNAGE, SIGNS, STATIONERY, STORES, STYLE, TASTE, TEAM, VALUE, VEHICLES

Count on It!

T	R	E	D	R	O	H	D	I	M	E	B	I	V	R
E	N	A	L	E	S	S	O	N	R	A	L	L	O	D
E	E	E	T	A	L	U	C	L	A	C	T	T	T	L
H	T	H	C	C	L	O	N	E	T	P	H	E	I
S	L	U	T	H	O	S	N	N	A	P	R	A	S	H
D	E	E	O	C	G	I	S	X	R	D	P	A	C	C
N	X	L	K	R	O	U	R	O	S	A	Y	R	H	K
O	P	R	E	C	S	O	F	G	O	L	A	T	A	C
C	E	E	N	C	I	I	I	T	A	M	L	T	L	Y
E	N	T	G	R	T	N	N	R	D	R	E	K	S
S	S	U	E	R	R	C	I	F	F	A	R	T	B	M
S	E	P	O	O	O	D	T	L	C	Y	I	A	O	A
N	U	M	B	E	R	W	E	K	O	S	T	N	A	R
S	A	O	A	A	R	S	T	L	U	S	E	R	R	T
N	T	C	C	G	E	R	A	H	S	Y	T	I	D	E

BELLS, CALCULATE, CARDINAL, CASH, CATALOG, CENSUS, CENT, CHALKBOARD, CHART, CHILD, CLOCK, CLONE, COIN, COMPUTER, DAYS, DIME, DOLLAR, ERROR, EXPENSE, FINITE, GAME, GREENS, GROWTH, HEAD, LESSON, LOST, MARCH, MATH, MONEY, NICKEL, NUMBER, ORDER, PACK, PRAY, PROFIT, REACH, RESULTS, ROBOT, ROMAN, ROUTE, SCALE, SECONDS, SELECT, SHARE, SHEET, SMART, SUPERIOR, TABS, TAX, TIDE, TOKEN, TRACK, TRAFFIC, TRAIN, VOTES

133

Crime Fighters

Solution: 6 letters

N	O	I	T	U	C	E	S	O	R	P	L	A	N	P
S	R	E	D	R	O	T	L	E	G	A	L	R	R	P
O	G	Y	T	E	F	A	S	T	E	S	T	O	T	L
J	U	R	Y	E	N	R	O	T	T	A	O	R	C	F
T	R	U	O	C	L	T	S	R	I	F	O	R	O	F
R	D	N	O	I	S	S	I	M	R	F	I	E	D	I
I	R	E	V	H	F	I	O	F	F	E	N	C	E	T
A	A	I	E	I	A	G	P	E	Y	T	Y	C	S	N
L	C	L	G	D	C	A	U	S	E	F	S	W	L	I
A	P	H	O	C	T	M	J	A	I	L	T	O	A	A
R	T	L	A	R	S	B	M	N	R	I	H	R	W	L
C	A	S	O	R	E	L	E	U	P	D	G	K	S	P
E	E	L	A	T	G	H	L	S	T	R	I	C	T	E
N	L	W	A	N	T	E	D	A	T	F	R	A	U	D
Y	P	T	R	U	S	T	S	E	C	A	G	E	N	T

ACES, AGENT, ATTORNEY, BEST, CALL, CARD, CASE, CAUSE, CHARGES, CIVIL, CODES, COURT, DEED, DRUG, EFFORT, ERROR, FACTS, FIGHT, FINE, FIRST, FRAUD, GUARDIAN, HELP, HERO, IDENTIFY, JAIL, JURY, LARCENY, LAWS, LAWYER, LEGAL, MAGISTRATE, MISSION, OFFENCE, ORDERS, PATROL, PLAINTIFF, PLAN, PLEA, PLOT, PROOF, PROSECUTION, RIGHTS, RULES, SAFETY, STRICT, TEAM, TEST, TIPS, TRIAL, TRUST, WANTED, WARS, WORK

Dancing on Ice

Solution: 11 letters

S	D	P	L	E	M	G	R	S	S	W	I	F	T	S
R	U	L	L	L	L	E	G	M	O	D	A	A	S	E
A	E	Y	A	I	I	N	R	U	C	S	U	N	E	T
T	T	C	D	N	I	K	G	I	T	I	R	C	C	A
S	W	I	S	C	O	R	S	D	T	U	S	Y	N	K
C	N	I	N	E	A	I	D	A	T	S	T	U	A	S
G	I	A	R	C	R	R	S	T	S	C	P	U	M	A
C	D	L	E	L	I	U	S	S	O	O	D	O	R	T
N	H	F	B	V	S	T	G	S	E	I	L	E	O	H
I	U	A	E	U	O	S	T	I	E	F	N	O	F	L
L	W	M	R	O	P	U	G	N	F	A	O	O	R	E
S	O	O	B	M	M	H	C	U	S	N	H	R	E	T
T	H	S	U	E	T	E	R	A	L	U	P	O	P	E
C	S	J	S	S	R	E	C	U	D	O	R	P	P	S
A	O	R	C	H	E	S	T	R	A	S	N	I	P	S

ACTS, ARENAS, ATHLETES, AUDIENCE, BOOTS, CHARM, CHORUS, COSTUMES, DANCING, DRIVE, DUET, EIGHTS, FANCY, FAST, FIGURES, GLIDING, GRACEFUL, HOPS, JUMPS, LOOPS, MERIT, MUSIC, NUMBERS, ORCHESTRAS, PERFORMANCES, POPULAR, PRODUCERS, PROFESSIONAL, PUBLIC, SHOW, SKATES, SKILL, SOLO, SPINS, STADIUMS, STARS, STYLE, SUCH, SWIFT, TURNS, TWIRLS

135

Driving Schools

Solution: 8 letters

T	N	N	U	F	S	S	A	P	N	J	R	P	R	I
R	F	I	A	A	T	C	A	A	U	M	S	A	N	L
T	U	I	G	W	S	C	I	D	E	R	N	S	I	I
E	L	L	H	H	E	R	G	R	O	O	T	A	T	N
S	S	E	E	S	T	M	G	R	I	R	T	H	O	L
L	E	N	K	S	E	E	R	T	U	S	G	I	I	C
L	C	N	E	N	L	I	A	C	U	I	T	N	V	O
I	O	D	T	C	M	N	T	R	A	C	E	E	I	N
H	E	T	I	B	I	O	T	R	E	S	I	E	E	T
P	S	H	R	M	R	L	T	S	M	V	P	T	W	R
E	E	A	A	A	A	S	R	O	N	E	E	E	Y	O
V	K	X	L	N	F	E	E	E	R	O	D	R	E	L
E	E	A	G	F	T	F	E	M	N	I	L	I	S	D
N	N	I	O	N	A	R	I	P	O	T	S	Y	A	E
E	S	G	I	S	G	T	S	C	O	R	E	T	P	N

BRAKE, CITY, CONTROL, EVEN, EXAMINATION, FAIL, FLASH, FOG,
FUN, GREEN, HILLS, HONK, INSTRUCTOR, INTERSECTION, JUDGMENT,
LANE, LICENSE, LINES, MEDIAN, MERGE, MIRRORS, MOTORIST, NIGHT,
PACE, PASS, PEDESTRIAN, PERMIT, PYLONS, RAIN, RENT, REVERSE,
RULES, SAFE, SCORE, SHIFT, SIGNAL, SPEED, STEER, STOP, STRAIGHT,
TAIL, TEST, TRAFFIC, TRUST, VEHICLE, VIEW, WHEEL

Extreme Sports

Solution: 6 letters

S	R	F	G	W	I	N	T	E	R	J	O	U	S	T
S	E	E	A	N	R	U	G	B	Y	U	U	K	R	C
E	T	V	G	S	I	A	E	N	T	E	A	D	A	I
S	E	N	A	N	T	K	K	S	I	T	K	E	G	T
S	S	R	E	S	A	L	I	G	E	T	R	C	E	E
O	T	T	R	V	I	D	H	B	N	A	F	N	O	L
R	O	I	O	F	E	P	O	S	D	I	P	A	R	H
C	F	M	T	I	D	A	R	I	N	G	P	L	R	T
A	H	I	E	L	R	R	C	R	F	K	P	A	A	A
L	N	A	I	D	E	A	A	A	A	A	C	B	E	D
G	U	M	I	C	L	C	H	P	L	D	I	O	E	L
E	I	N	O	N	E	H	M	C	L	L	W	X	L	U
T	G	R	G	S	S	U	K	O	I	A	I	I	R	C
O	D	U	J	E	J	T	C	T	N	M	L	N	A	K
S	A	I	L	L	L	E	Y	T	G	E	D	G	G	Y

ABILITY, ATHLETIC, BALANCE, BIKING, BOXING, CALLING, CHAINS, CHARIOTS, CLAP, CLOCK, COLD, DANGER, DARING, DEMO, EVENTS, FALLING, FAST, FIRST, HIKE, HOCKEY, JOUST, JUDGE, JUDO, JUMP, LACROSSE, LASERS, LEAPING, LIFTING, LIMIT, LUCKY, LUGE, LUNGE, MIXED, OUTSIDE, PARACHUTE, RACES, RADICAL, RAFTING, RAGE, RAPIDS, RECORD, RUGBY, SAIL, SAVES, SKATEBOARDING, STAGE, TITLE, WAVES, WILD, WINTER, YELL

137

Falconry

T	F	W	A	T	C	H	R	E	S	H	E	N	S	S
T	E	L	T	N	U	A	G	W	C	E	R	Y	P	S
C	A	R	R	Y	I	G	E	R	C	A	A	E	O	E
E	T	E	R	S	S	M	E	N	E	O	C	R	R	S
L	H	L	E	I	P	P	A	L	F	I	U	P	T	I
G	E	E	E	U	T	T	D	L	E	I	F	R	E	C
A	R	A	R	R	S	O	Y	S	H	U	N	T	S	R
E	S	S	I	T	I	R	M	C	P	A	R	T	E	
L	U	E	D	H	N	S	E	Y	A	L	L	A	C	X
E	O	Y	E	G	H	T	E	T	T	R	I	N	A	E
N	A	R	I	C	H	C	I	K	T	L	R	D	G	P
S	I	R	T	O	H	E	N	R	A	U	L	L	E	B
H	E	A	D	N	N	A	O	U	T	D	O	O	R	E
O	C	U	R	C	O	P	S	E	A	V	T	H	O	A
W	R	Q	E	T	E	C	R	E	E	L	P	E	E	K

ATTACH, BEAK, BELL, CAGE, CALL, CARE, CARRY, CATCH, CHASE, CONTROL, COURSE, DISTANCE, EAGLE, EGGS, EXERCISES, FEATHERS, FIELD, FLYING, GAUNTLET, GLOVE, HEAD, HOLD, HUNT, KEEP, KESTREL, LAUNCH, LEARN, LEASH, METHOD, MEWS, OUTDOOR, PATIENCE, PERCH, PREY, PURSUE, QUARRY, RAISE, RELEASE, RETURN, ROPE, SHOW, SPECIES, SPORT, TAIL, TERRITORY, TEST, TIED, TRAIN, TRAP, WATCH

Fall Is Here

D	S	E	S	S	A	L	C	G	S	Y	A	L	P	J
N	F	Y	E	K	C	O	H	N	O	P	S	I	O	F
I	H	A	I	L	L	U	I	I	U	E	O	G	P	R
W	C	R	R	L	N	K	P	K	P	C	G	R	E	A
Y	I	L	E	T	P	E	P	A	O	I	H	L	T	C
T	R	G	O	M	I	N	C	R	N	V	O	A	S	S
I	E	A	U	U	M	S	N	G	E	O	L	L	R	W
S	S	P	V	U	D	U	T	G	C	F	R	E	E	T
R	U	E	T	N	C	S	E	S	C	A	A	A	S	H
E	M	U	A	O	S	T	K	L	C	S	T	V	M	E
V	A	L	P	S	A	E	O	Y	L	H	C	E	E	A
I	I	I	G	B	O	T	E	L	E	I	O	S	L	T
N	A	E	L	Y	H	N	I	R	T	O	A	O	T	E
U	C	E	W	E	M	H	A	Y	T	N	T	P	L	R
E	S	S	S	S	C	S	A	L	E	S	S	G	O	L

ARTISTS, AUTUMN, CHART, CHILL, CITY, CLASSES, CLOTHES, CLOUDS, COATS, COLLEGE, COOLER, CORNUCOPIA, FASHIONS, GYMS, HAIL, HOCKEY, HUNT, JOGGING, LANDSCAPES, LEAVES, LOGS, MUSE, PANORAMA, PETS, PLAYS, POSE, PUMPKINS, RAKING, RICH, SALES, SCARF, SCHOOL, SEASONAL, SKY, SMELT, SOUP, SPORTS, THEATER, TREES, UNIVERSITY, VARY, VEGETABLES, VIEWS, WEATHER, WIND

139

Feeling Numb

Solution: 7 letters

T	F	O	O	T	T	U	O	B	T	S	I	R	W	C
R	S	R	P	A	T	I	E	N	T	P	S	U	I	C
E	E	E	E	D	C	D	E	N	T	I	S	T	N	R
D	B	L	R	E	S	I	I	S	A	H	O	Y	J	E
N	S	U	A	P	Z	D	G	P	F	C	L	U	E	A
U	G	P	T	X	A	E	C	R	R	I	K	Z	C	M
S	B	M	I	L	L	I	I	A	A	O	A	C	T	E
D	E	B	O	N	E	S	N	D	I	H	T	N	A	S
E	H	O	N	S	A	G	O	K	D	S	T	E	L	B
T	E	C	T	C	N	C	T	E	I	K	C	E	N	L
A	A	A	U	I	T	L	T	C	L	L	E	D	L	L
D	T	R	B	O	Y	L	K	I	I	P	L	L	A	I
E	E	B	R	I	T	O	M	O	V	E	M	E	N	T
S	U	C	N	O	I	S	I	V	E	E	H	D	R	S
R	E	G	I	O	N	T	L	U	F	E	C	A	E	P

AFRAID, BACK, BEDS, BONES, BOUT, CREAM, CURE, DAILY, DENTIST, DOCTOR, DRUGS, FOOT, FREEZE, HAZE, HEAL, HEAT, HIPS, ICED, INACTIVE, INJECT, LEGS, LETHARGIC, LIMBS, LIVE, LOST, LYING, MOVEMENT, NARCOTIC, NECK, NEEDLE, OPERATION, PAINKILLER, PATIENT, PEACEFUL, REGION, RELAX, REST, RUBBING, SEDATED, SICK, SLEEP, SPIN, STATE, STILL, TOES, TONIC, TORPID, TOUCH, UNDER, VISION, VOICE, WRIST

Food Sales

Solution: 10 letters

N	S	T	U	C	A	U	S	E	Y	P	I	E	S	S
O	R	L	F	O	A	S	G	N	I	D	D	U	P	E
M	R	A	E	M	N	K	N	N	M	O	N	E	Y	T
E	H	G	G	M	S	I	E	U	I	R	E	A	S	R
L	C	O	A	U	A	H	S	S	B	K	O	N	C	O
S	A	O	U	N	S	R	O	I	P	R	O	F	I	T
E	E	D	Y	I	I	B	A	R	A	I	N	O	M	A
T	P	L	R	T	U	Z	S	C	T	R	C	U	C	R
I	L	A	B	Y	S	M	A	A	D	B	F	E	R	T
R	P	O	S	A	E	A	I	T	A	F	R	I	S	S
O	S	D	O	T	T	C	T	E	I	F	C	E	C	E
V	S	E	I	K	O	O	C	N	D	O	U	O	A	B
A	Y	E	A	S	T	K	S	A	T	A	N	D	S	D
F	E	F	S	P	U	O	R	G	R	E	M	S	G	T
E	K	A	C	T	R	O	H	S	S	L	L	O	R	E

ASSOCIATIONS, BEST, BUNS, BUYS, CAKES, CANDY, CARAMELS, CAUSE, COMMUNITY, COOKIES, COOKING, COST, CUTS, FAVORITES, FEED, FORM, FUDGE, GOOD, GROUPS, ITEMS, KEEP, LEMON, LOOK, MADE, MONEY, MUFFINS, ORGANIZATIONS, PARISH, PEACH, PIES, PROFIT, PUDDINGS, RAISIN, ROLLS, SCONES, SHORTBREAD, SHORTCAKE, SPICES, SUGAR, TABLES, TARTS, TASK, TASTY, TORTES, YEAST

141

Footprints of Extinct Animals

Solution: 15 letters

S	P	C	I	S	S	A	I	R	T	S	S	G	F	S
S	U	L	I	M	B	S	T	S	U	A	U	N	A	T
S	L	O	E	O	S	T	R	O	S	T	R	I	D	E
L	D	I	R	T	Z	U	R	S	E	E	U	K	E	P
S	N	I	S	O	A	O	C	I	S	S	A	R	U	J
T	I	E	N	S	V	R	S	Z	O	T	S	A	P	S
I	K	D	O	I	O	I	B	E	S	C	O	M	K	E
G	N	N	N	S	M	F	B	E	M	A	L	C	T	N
I	I	R	S	I	O	O	D	R	T	F	A	A	T	O
D	A	E	L	O	H	I	H	G	E	R	G	E	W	B
C	D	N	A	I	M	R	E	P	T	H	E	A	L	S
S	G	E	L	E	R	O	F	F	I	F	M	V	I	A
A	O	R	N	I	T	H	O	P	O	D	S	S	A	T
N	T	T	C	R	E	T	A	C	E	O	U	S	R	A
D	S	N	A	I	B	I	H	P	M	A	T	S	T	D

AMPHIBIANS, BONES, CARNIVOROUS, CLAWS, CRETACEOUS, CROSSED, DATA, DIGITS, DINOSAURS, FACT, FADE, FEET, FOOT, FORELEGS, FOSSILS, GAIT, HERBIVOROUS, HIND, HOMINIDS, JURASSIC, KIND, LIMBS, MARKING, MEGALOSAURUS, MESOZOIC, ORNITHOPODS, PAST, PERMIAN, SAND, SEDIMENTS, SIZE, SORTS, STEP, TEST, TOES, TRACKS, TRAIL, TRIASSIC, VERTEBRATE

Fundraisers

Solution: 11 letters

D	H	F	H	O	T	H	N	U	S	C	S	N	D	S
N	S	S	D	E	G	O	O	E	O	E	S	O	R	E
A	A	S	L	E	I	A	I	M	H	A	R	E	B	U
B	C	L	L	T	D	N	M	C	E	C	E	R	S	D
S	A	O	A	A	O	I	R	E	H	H	E	U	I	R
B	N	N	M	H	T	U	C	E	C	A	T	N	T	O
S	O	O	P	M	H	I	S	A	K	A	N	I	V	S
D	T	M	E	C	I	T	P	F	T	E	U	O	C	N
S	Y	N	R	H	R	T	A	S	R	I	L	S	H	O
S	T	A	U	A	C	S	T	S	O	U	O	E	E	P
S	M	I	S	O	T	N	A	E	M	H	V	N	C	S
U	O	A	K	S	M	R	U	E	E	E	T	I	K	N
P	L	E	D	G	E	A	S	L	N	S	G	S	E	S
E	S	C	O	P	E	V	I	T	C	E	J	B	O	W
R	T	R	O	P	P	U	S	C	I	T	I	L	O	P

AMOUNTS, BALLET, BAND, BASH, BREAKFASTS, CASH, CAUSES,
CHECK, CHEERS, CHURCHES, COMMITMENT, COMMITTEES,
DEDICATION, DINNERS, DONATION, DUES, EVENTS, GAME, GEMS,
HOME, HOSPITALS, KITS, LUNCHEONS, MARCH, OBJECTIVE, OPERA,
ORCHESTRAS, PLEDGE, POLITICS, POST, SALE, SCOPE, SPONSOR,
STATUS, SUPER, SUPPORT, SYMPHONIES, VIEW, VOLUMES,
VOLUNTEERS

143

Garage Sales

L	S	T	J	T	S	E	V	S	T	O	P	D	G	S
A	S	E	S	E	R	I	O	M	R	A	A	E	N	E
M	S	R	L	E	W	H	I	S	K	E	C	S	I	H
P	H	B	E	I	R	E	T	S	S	E	K	U	H	S
S	A	B	V	C	T	C	L	N	R	A	T	C	T	I
T	D	I	R	A	U	E	I	S	T	E	T	U	O	D
G	E	R	B	D	S	A	R	E	S	A	T	P	L	R
N	S	C	O	E	G	E	S	U	B	I	E	S	C	F
I	L	R	U	R	N	T	I	L	T	Y	L	H	O	P
D	P	R	A	R	A	E	E	T	R	I	A	V	L	P
D	R	B	E	T	T	C	F	E	I	I	N	A	E	S
E	I	A	U	P	L	A	T	I	R	L	T	R	A	R
B	S	E	P	O	P	T	I	S	T	E	I	F	U	X
O	S	O	T	E	O	O	C	N	S	S	O	T	O	F
R	S	H	H	P	S	K	C	A	S	S	S	B	U	T

ARMOIRES, BARGAINS, BEDDING, BENEFITS, BOX, CHAIRS, CLOTHING, COPPER, CREST, CRIB, CUPS, CURTAINS, DISHES, DRAPES, FLUTE, FURNITURE, HOSE, JEWELS, LAMPS, PACK, PLATES, POSTERS, POTS, POTTERY, PRODUCTS, ROBE, ROCKERS, SACKS, SAUCERS, SHADES, SILVER, SKATES, SOFAS, STATUES, TABLECLOTH, TABLES, TILES, TUBS, USED, UTILITIES, VASE, VEST, WHISK

Get Out Your Skates

S	E	T	A	K	S	G	H	E	W	E	L	O	B	D
C	P	E	S	N	N	N	R	S	Q	I	U	E	S	L
O	M	I	S	I	R	U	E	U	A	T	N	G	O	O
S	R	S	D	I	S	U	I	R	D	D	N	D	L	C
B	E	I	R	A	C	P	T	O	D	I	U	R	O	S
P	L	R	E	E	M	R	O	W	T	L	E	L	R	C
G	A	L	U	E	V	R	E	A	O	L	I	E	T	I
E	P	G	N	G	S	I	R	X	A	S	N	H	N	S
V	C	T	N	D	I	O	R	X	E	T	O	D	C	U
E	N	A	N	I	G	F	A	U	R	B	O	M	B	M
N	S	O	F	I	T	T	M	A	P	O	O	L	E	R
I	P	E	V	R	I	S	P	I	R	A	A	O	I	S
N	I	N	K	O	U	O	A	S	T	D	R	N	T	N
G	I	D	N	A	T	S	S	O	E	T	K	K	H	S
S	Y	A	D	I	L	O	H	S	C	S	S	I	S	P

ADULTS, BEND, BLADES, BOOTS, BRISK, CHILDREN, COASTING, COLD, COLISEUMS, DASH, DIPS, EQUIPMENT, EVENINGS, EXERCISE, FIGURES, GLIDING, HOLIDAYS, INDOORS, INVIGORATING, LAKES, MITTS, MUSIC, OUTDOORS, PARKS, PARTNERS, PLEASURE, PONDS, RELAXATION, RINKS, RIVERS, SKATES, SOLO, STAND, SURFACE, TRAIL, TURN, TWOSOMES, WIND

145

Giving a Helping Hand

Solution: 7 letters

S	G	D	H	C	C	N	F	S	D	N	A	H	E	M
W	I	N	E	U	H	O	A	E	A	S	H	Z	O	I
T	A	G	I	P	R	I	S	L	S	F	I	N	Y	N
K	N	R	N	M	P	T	L	I	P	N	E	H	E	D
S	G	E	M	I	I	A	S	D	A	Y	T	E	E	A
A	N	M	I	T	D	T	C	G	R	R	D	T	R	G
T	I	I	U	T	H	R	R	I	O	E	C	O	U	F
H	R	T	R	T	A	O	A	W	D	I	N	I	O	P
E	E	I	R	O	O	P	E	W	L	N	D	C	A	F
A	F	L	A	L	Y	S	E	F	E	A	A	R	C	S
R	F	F	P	L	I	N	F	V	N	R	E	H	E	S
T	U	I	E	A	S	A	T	C	E	N	A	S	V	E
S	S	N	R	C	S	R	E	E	T	N	U	L	O	V
H	O	P	E	S	T	T	H	S	G	A	T	Y	L	O
L	P	A	L	S	I	C	K	E	C	C	A	S	E	M

AFFLICTED, ASSIST, CARE, CASE, CAUSES, CHANGE, CHEER, CHILDREN, DESTITUTE, EFFECT, EVENTS, FOOD, FORM, FREE, GUIDANCE, HANDICAPPED, HANDS, HEARTS, HELP, HOPES, HURT, LONELY, LOVE, MIND, MONEY, MOVES, NEED, ORGANIZE, PALS, PARENTS, PATIENT, PLAN, POOR, PRAISEWORTHY, REWARDING, SAFE, SICK, SIGN, SUFFERING, TASK, TIME, TIMING, TOLL, TRANSPORTATION, TRIALS, VOLUNTEERS, WARMTH

Golden

Solution: 6 letters

J	S	T	A	D	O	R	N	M	E	N	T	S	U	D
E	S	L	N	B	L	A	C	K	D	D	W	F	D	S
W	O	L	L	E	Y	Y	B	Y	L	L	H	O	P	E
E	L	I	A	E	M	D	W	T	I	O	O	R	R	L
L	G	F	N	E	P	E	N	U	G	G	E	T	O	C
R	R	O	H	O	I	N	L	A	Y	I	A	U	S	I
Y	M	C	H	G	C	T	R	E	I	R	W	N	P	T
P	L	S	H	T	S	I	U	B	A	A	R	E	E	R
A	L	T	L	O	N	S	S	K	T	M	N	A	C	A
B	G	A	A	G	V	T	H	C	M	O	L	D	T	P
A	T	N	T	N	E	R	H	I	I	C	I	E	I	S
R	S	D	E	I	I	Y	B	L	N	L	O	A	N	P
S	A	A	M	O	N	A	L	L	O	Y	F	L	G	A
H	O	R	E	C	N	U	O	S	A	D	I	M	O	C
T	C	D	E	K	B	E	M	B	R	O	I	D	E	R

ADORNMENT, ALCHEMY, ALLOY, BANK, BARS, BEAUTY, BLACK,
BULLION, CAPS, COAST, COIN, COLOR, CROWN, DEAL, DENTISTRY,
DUST, ELEMENT, EMBROIDER, FILL, FOIL, FORTUNE, GILD, GLOSS,
GOOD, HOPE, INGOT, INLAY, JEWELRY, KARAT, LEAF, MARIGOLD,
METAL, MIDAS, MOLD, MONEY, NUGGET, OLYMPICS, OUNCE,
PARTICLES, PLATINUM, PROSPECTING, RARE, RING, RUSH, SHINY,
SHOP, SOLID, STANDARD, STAR, VEIN, WATCH, WEIGHT, YELLOW

147

Guide to Mushrooms

Solution: 11 letters

L	C	E	H	Y	P	H	A	E	C	K	C	A	L	B
A	L	A	E	A	B	L	U	L	E	H	U	M	U	S
R	W	A	P	R	B	I	A	S	A	T	C	T	D	R
G	A	O	M	S	T	I	T	N	E	D	I	B	L	E
E	R	D	L	S	S	D	T	T	T	R	P	H	I	G
K	N	L	I	G	U	E	S	A	E	D	O	O	W	N
L	I	O	S	N	R	C	D	T	T	R	C	P	B	A
A	N	M	C	E	A	O	W	V	E	A	S	R	S	D
T	G	S	L	I	O	M	E	E	S	M	O	R	P	N
S	L	L	S	F	X	P	E	C	D	W	R	O	U	U
D	E	L	I	C	I	O	U	S	N	L	C	D	O	O
A	R	I	Z	C	A	S	T	T	W	I	I	O	R	R
R	O	G	E	P	O	I	S	O	N	M	M	M	G	G
K	M	R	O	F	O	N	R	N	U	C	L	E	U	S
M	Y	C	O	L	O	G	Y	H	N	F	R	E	S	H

ASCUS, BITTER, BLACK, BROWN, CAPS, CHANTERELLE, DANGER, DARK, DECOMPOSING, DELICIOUS, EDIBLE, FOOD, FORM, FRESH, GILLS, GLOW, GROUND, GROUPS, GROW, HABITAT, HUMID, HUMUS, HYPHAE, LARGE, MICROSCOPIC, MILDEW, MOLD, MOREL, MYCOLOGY, NAMES, NUCLEUS, ODOR, PLANT, POISON, RECIPE, RUST, SIZE, SMALL, SOIL, SPORES, STALK, STEM, TOXIC, TREE, WARNING, WHITE, WILD, WOOD

Handmade Stuff

Solution: 8 letters

C	O	N	T	R	A	S	T	L	T	E	G	D	A	G
F	E	O	M	A	M	N	T	S	E	S	L	P	D	E
I	U	C	S	O	I	A	M	F	K	T	P	B	R	M
G	L	I	M	A	T	E	R	I	A	L	S	L	A	S
U	G	L	P	H	T	I	L	I	Y	R	S	A	W	T
R	E	R	E	O	E	L	F	N	O	P	C	N	P	A
I	O	A	T	B	N	M	A	S	K	N	I	K	E	H
N	R	F	S	B	S	G	S	T	B	T	E	E	S	P
E	I	O	J	Y	L	I	F	R	A	C	S	T	C	E
N	G	R	N	A	C	F	E	U	S	R	K	A	T	E
A	I	M	S	S	R	T	M	M	E	E	R	D	F	E
M	N	S	M	C	O	S	T	E	B	W	O	O	L	B
E	A	O	Y	U	L	M	A	N	Y	O	W	O	H	S
L	L	E	C	O	L	O	R	T	W	L	S	P	U	C
D	E	H	S	E	T	A	E	R	C	F	T	S	E	B

APPLY, APRON, BASE, BELL, BEST, BLANKET, COLOR, CONTRAST, COST, CRAFTS, CREATE, CUPS, DRAW, EASY, EMBOSS, ENAMEL, FAST, FIGURINE, FLOWER, FORM, GADGET, GEMS, GIFT, GLASS, GLUE, HATS, HOBBY, ICON, INSTRUMENT, IRON, JARS, MANY, MARIONETTE, MASK, MATERIAL, MITTENS, MOLD, MOTIF, ORIGINAL, PAINT, PASTEL, PENS, PIECE, RETOUCH, SCARF, SCISSORS, SEAM, SHOW, SKILL, TABLE, TOTEMS, TOYS, WOOD, WOOL, WORK

149

Hybrid Corn Production

Solution: 10 letters

Y	T	I	L	I	B	A	L	I	A	V	A	S	Y	Y
C	C	M	R	A	F	E	C	O	B	S	E	S	R	I
G	R	O	W	E	R	S	N	A	R	R	M	N	E	E
S	V	O	M	E	S	T	S	E	U	S	E	O	S	L
T	S	A	P	M	E	E	C	T	F	O	R	I	R	D
R	N	Y	R	X	E	U	A	M	I	I	I	T	U	I
A	T	E	T	I	D	R	A	R	Q	L	T	I	N	M
I	U	U	M	O	E	R	C	U	C	E	L	D	C	E
N	R	C	R	P	K	T	A	I	S	H	U	N	E	T
E	D	P	M	E	O	L	I	T	A	S	E	O	T	H
E	S	E	T	A	I	L	I	E	T	L	S	C	A	O
H	T	I	R	T	N	E	R	S	S	T	L	M	D
I	N	S	I	B	G	I	I	V	E	N	I	L	I	S
G	H	E	A	T	N	A	N	K	E	R	N	E	L	S
H	S	U	P	T	L	I	F	G	U	D	U	S	C	L

AVAILABILITY, BASE, BENEFIT, CLIMATE, COBS, COMMERCIAL, CONDITIONS, CROP, DEVELOPMENT, FARM, GROWERS, HEAT, HIGH, INBRED, INDUSTRIAL, KERNELS, LINE, MARKETING, MATING, MERIT, METHODS, NURSERY, PRODUCERS, PUSH, QUALITIES, RESEARCH, SELL, SOIL, STRAIN, TASTE, TEMPERATURES, TESTING, TEXTURE, TILL, TYPE, UNITS, VARIETIES, YIELD

Imagining UFOs

Solution: 7 letters

E	P	A	C	S	E	S	F	N	D	D	G	O	N	E
S	L	S	P	A	C	E	O	N	E	N	R	O	S	S
C	A	M	E	R	A	I	E	E	I	A	I	E	C	C
S	N	T	A	R	T	G	P	D	D	S	R	I	A	A
F	E	F	E	P	E	S	N	S	U	I	E	B	R	M
H	T	P	E	L	T	A	M	L	H	N	V	M	Y	S
P	A	C	O	C	L	S	L	I	C	I	O	E	C	L
A	E	P	E	H	I	I	S	E	H	R	P	S	W	E
R	L	J	P	N	O	E	T	C	R	O	S	S	E	S
G	B	I	A	E	R	S	R	E	C	T	S	A	I	S
O	S	G	E	U	N	A	T	S	I	E	W	G	R	E
T	R	E	T	N	E	I	E	I	S	O	O	E	D	V
O	A	C	I	S	S	L	N	I	L	N	T	S	O	L
H	I	L	E	K	E	S	O	G	R	E	P	O	R	T
P	S	R	E	T	S	N	O	M	A	R	T	I	A	N

ALIENS, ARMOR, CAMERA, CRAFT, CROSSES, DREAM, ESCAPE, FEAR, GLOW, GONE, HAPPENING, HOPES, HOSTILE, ILLUSION, LANDING, LEGEND, LOST, MARTIAN, MESSAGES, MONSTERS, NEARBY, NOISES, OBJECTS, ORGANISMS, PHOTOGRAPH, PICTURES, PLANET, RECEPTION, REPORT, RESEARCH, SAILS, SATELLITE, SCAMS, SCARY, SCIENCE, SHIPS, SKIES, SPACE, SPEED, TALE, TELESCOPE, VESSEL, VIDEOS, WEIRD

151

In the Pink

N	R	E	T	T	A	P	S	R	B	S	S	E	R	D
H	S	H	T	O	U	E	I	L	O	D	P	O	P	C
S	K	C	O	I	I	O	O	L	W	S	S	I	A	H
I	L	M	I	D	U	S	R	B	S	E	N	R	L	E
L	A	E	N	R	S	R	E	T	S	K	N	I	P	E
O	H	A	W	O	B	L	F	S	I	A	N	I	S	K
P	C	T	M	E	T	A	S	E	T	C	G	I	B	S
E	D	S	L	S	J	O	F	I	P	S	L	U	P	H
T	N	I	T	U	L	F	O	P	S	A	L	M	O	N
R	T	I	I	F	L	N	O	R	D	B	R	G	T	E
O	I	C	V	O	S	P	S	Y	K	S	S	G	S	Y
C	E	B	W	K	C	E	R	N	L	N	S	E	K	P
E	D	E	B	O	N	O	P	I	N	K	I	N	G	I
D	R	R	R	O	C	I	A	O	I	K	I	P	N	L
S	S	N	C	B	N	N	P	N	S	P	E	A	R	L

BELTS, BLOSSOM, BOOK, BOWS, BULB, CAKES, CANDIES, CARNATIONS, CHALK, CHEEKS, CONES, CORYDALIS, DECOR, DRESS, FABRICS, FLOSS, FLOWERS, GRAPEFRUIT, HOGS, JEWELS, JUICE, LIPS, MEATS, NAILS, PATTERN, PEARL, PIGS, PILL, PINKIE, PINKING, PINKROOT, PINK SLIP, PINKSTER, PINK VINE, PINKY, POLISH, POPCORN, POTS, RIBBON, ROSES, SALMON, SKIES, SKIN, TILE, TINT, TROUT

152

Keyboarding

Solution: 9 letters

T	P	E	V	I	T	U	C	E	X	E	G	A	P	G
F	A	R	E	T	U	P	M	O	C	S	T	B	N	N
I	A	R	K	C	A	B	Y	A	L	P	E	K	O	O
H	R	O	O	N	A	I	P	O	I	A	N	S	I	S
S	R	R	O	S	W	S	C	L	T	L	R	E	T	N
C	O	O	B	C	N	K	E	T	E	L	E	D	C	O
R	W	F	E	O	I	S	R	L	L	A	T	S	N	I
E	S	D	T	N	E	M	U	R	T	S	N	I	U	T
E	O	T	O	W	S	S	O	R	R	N	I	Z	F	C
N	U	O	N	P	A	L	C	N	E	E	O	E	I	U
B	T	G	U	R	V	R	O	A	O	V	T	F	N	R
R	L	G	M	I	E	P	E	O	P	G	O	N	G	T
E	E	L	B	N	Y	Y	R	A	T	E	R	C	E	S
A	T	E	E	T	Y	P	E	W	R	I	T	E	R	N
K	S	D	R	O	C	S	R	E	K	A	E	P	S	I

ARROWS, BEAT, BREAK, BUTTONS, COMPUTER, CORD, COVER, DELETE, DESK, ENTER, ERGONOMIC, ERROR, ESCAPE, EXECUTIVE, FINGERS, FONT, FUNCTION, INSTALL, INSTRUCTIONS, INSTRUMENT, INTERNET, LOCK, MAIL, NOTEBOOK, NUMBER, OUTLET, PAGE, PIANO, PILES, PLAYBACK, PRINT, SAVE, SCREEN, SECRETARY, SHIFT, SIZE, SOFTWARE, SONG, SPEAKERS, TOGGLE, TOOLS, TYPEWRITER, TYPO

153

Let's Tie Knots

Solution: 5 letters

P	C	R	E	E	F	S	S	S	T	P	N	P	U	E
H	O	L	D	L	A	H	E	P	S	W	O	R	B	D
S	S	O	A	I	P	I	O	H	L	S	I	U	U	E
S	N	E	L	S	T	I	E	L	I	I	T	N	V	T
L	T	O	G	E	S	E	T	T	E	C	C	R	E	T
N	R	N	I	D	P	I	I	L	E	S	U	E	E	O
S	E	R	E	S	E	O	F	S	U	C	R	N	D	N
G	A	C	H	M	N	C	R	I	A	M	T	I	I	K
V	N	A	K	S	G	E	A	L	E	S	S	L	W	N
H	N	O	I	T	T	E	M	L	D	D	N	W	E	U
K	T	Z	R	N	I	O	S	I	R	N	O	O	A	N
L	E	A	I	T	D	E	K	H	D	E	C	B	V	T
S	T	Y	P	E	S	R	S	P	A	R	T	S	E	I
F	A	E	L	R	E	V	O	L	C	P	S	N	D	E
F	A	S	T	W	I	S	T	C	D	N	E	B	I	D

BEND, BOWLINE, CALM, CLASSIFIED, CLOVERLEAF, CONSTRUCTION, CORD, CURVE, DIMENSIONS, EDGES, ENDS, FAST, HOLD, HOLES, INTERLACED, INTERSECT, KIDS, LOOP, MODELS, MULTIPLE, NECKTIES, PATH, POSITIONS, REEF, SAILORS, SEGMENTS, SHAPE, SHEEPSHANK, SIZES, SPLICED, STRAPS, STRONG, TUBE, TURN, TWINE, TWIST, TYPE, UNKNOTTED, UNTIED, VARIETIES, WEAVED, WIDE

Life in the High Arctic

E	F	I	L	A	E	S	B	S	H	T	R	O	N	F
S	S	O	M	P	D	E	E	P	U	P	S	A	I	P
A	T	U	Y	V	A	A	D	O	E	N	E	S	T	A
B	S	I	C	R	A	H	N	L	I	C	H	E	N	S
K	C	A	S	H	A	S	A	A	O	Y	N	N	U	S
T	P	N	A	I	U	E	T	R	C	C	E	N	W	L
E	F	C	I	I	V	N	P	R	E	R	I	I	T	A
L	O	O	N	A	U	I	T	S	E	M	L	M	S	N
U	S	U	S	O	R	M	A	M	L	L	U	A	O	D
H	I	G	M	S	S	R	S	M	O	E	A	Z	R	E
T	G	L	O	B	I	E	E	W	E	S	I	E	F	M
R	H	P	R	D	L	L	X	T	A	R	N	G	R	A
A	T	O	R	L	N	F	S	O	O	O	I	O	H	G
E	F	L	E	G	D	I	R	H	F	N	T	C	W	S
Q	U	E	B	E	C	N	W	A	D	S	E	R	A	N

ALERT, AMERICA, BASE, BEARS, CANADA, CAPE, COLD, DAWN,
DEEP, DOGS, EARTH, ELFIN, ELLESMERE, ERMINES, FISH, FORBS,
FOSSILS, FOXES, FROST, GAME, HARE, HORIZON, HUNT, INUIT,
LAND, LICHENS, LIFE, LOON, MAZE, MINUS, MOSS, MOUNTAINS,
MUSK, NARES, NEST, NORSE, NORTH, OCEAN, PASS, PEARY, POLAR,
POLE, PUPS, QUEBEC, RIDGE, SEAL, SIGHT, SLEIGHS, SNOW, STORM,
SUNNY, TERRAIN, THULE, VAST, VISITS, WILLOW, WIND

155

London's Museums

Solution: 4 letters

S	S	G	M	A	N	K	I	N	D	E	M	O	D	E
R	G	M	O	E	D	Y	A	O	T	S	I	T	S	C
E	A	N	E	L	R	A	O	A	T	K	L	I	N	N
W	T	R	I	E	D	H	T	Y	S	R	I	A	O	E
O	G	H	L	T	D	L	P	A	N	O	T	R	I	I
T	K	L	N	L	N	E	U	W	O	W	A	T	T	C
D	A	O	I	O	R	I	A	A	I	B	R	R	C	S
G	R	H	O	C	G	L	A	M	T	V	Y	O	E	L
H	C	O	I	L	L	R	B	P	I	R	H	P	L	A
H	S	V	F	A	A	L	A	C	B	S	U	A	L	L
A	A	I	C	T	E	N	T	P	I	D	M	O	O	B
L	R	E	T	D	R	O	H	W	H	S	I	N	C	E
L	E	M	O	I	R	E	E	T	X	I	D	V	G	R
S	A	N	O	I	R	J	H	I	E	O	C	U	A	T
N	S	B	A	R	D	B	M	Y	N	B	H	O	L	D

ALBERT, AREAS, ARMOR, BARD, BETHNAL, BOAT, BRITISH, CHILDHOOD, COLLECTIONS, COURTAULD, DATA, DAVID, DOME, ETHNOGRAPHIC, EXHIBITIONS, GALLERY, GOLD, GREEN, HALLS, HERTFORD, HOLD, HUGE, JEWISH, LONDON, LOOK, MANKIND, MILITARY, MIX, PAINTINGS, PERCIVAL, PORTRAIT, SCIENCE, SMALL, TAGS, TATE, TOWERS, TYPE, VICTORIA, WALLACE, WIMBLEDON, WORKS

Mae West

Solution: 10 letters

E	K	C	I	W	H	S	U	B	S	C	C	S	F	S
L	V	D	N	E	G	E	L	E	L	A	O	H	U	T
E	V	I	T	A	C	O	V	O	R	P	M	P	E	A
V	S	O	R	M	N	O	T	S	S	M	E	A	N	G
E	O	T	L	D	L	H	H	O	U	R	D	R	T	E
N	L	I	E	U	E	A	T	N	S	O	I	G	R	M
A	I	O	C	S	P	O	I	T	B	L	E	O	A	Y
J	L	S	R	E	H	T	A	E	F	O	N	T	N	A
O	D	A	S	P	A	R	U	M	O	C	N	U	C	M
H	N	D	F	L	S	N	W	O	G	L	E	A	E	L
N	O	L	P	R	L	Y	A	V	U	A	C	D	S	O
O	M	I	L	A	A	A	N	I	I	S	N	E	W	B
V	A	T	A	T	U	N	C	E	D	T	A	I	O	M
A	I	A	C	W	A	L	K	S	O	S	D	R	O	Y
K	D	M	E	D	I	A	F	A	S	H	I	O	N	S

AUTOGRAPHS, BLONDE, BUSHWICK, CALLS, CLOTHES, COLOR, COMEDIENNE, DANCE, DEIRO, DIAMOND LIL, DRIVE, ENTRANCES, FASHIONS, FEATHERS, FRANK, GOWNS, GUIDO, JANE, JOHN, LASTS, LEGEND, LOVES, MATILDA, MAYME, MEDIA, MOVIES, NOVAK, PAUL, PHOTOS, PLACE, PLATINUM, PROVOCATIVE, ROLE, SETS, SHAPE, STAGE, SUPERSTAR, SWOON, SYMBOL, VOICE, VOLUPTUOUS, WALK

157

Mountain Climbing

Solution: 9 letters

S	T	H	D	D	A	E	L	G	C	S	E	P	O	R
H	F	N	S	L	E	D	R	L	L	R	Y	I	V	N
I	A	F	E	T	O	X	N	O	U	A	A	R	E	S
G	S	H	I	C	O	H	P	A	L	P	C	G	R	K
H	E	E	I	L	S	O	T	E	H	P	Y	I	L	I
K	C	A	P	K	C	A	B	O	D	X	X	L	A	L
Y	Z	O	R	O	E	S	T	A	O	I	A	E	A	L
A	R	I	N	U	L	O	N	P	L	F	T	D	R	R
C	S	E	C	D	G	S	E	O	E	A	V	I	E	E
K	A	S	N	R	I	V	M	S	P	E	N	H	O	T
R	E	R	A	E	E	T	P	G	N	M	T	C	T	N
R	A	P	E	R	C	I	I	T	U	A	A	S	E	I
D	H	N	E	A	K	S	U	O	E	I	O	R	C	W
Y	I	S	G	E	C	R	Q	W	N	O	D	Y	C	O
L	T	U	S	E	E	H	E	S	B	S	S	E	X	A

ADVENTURE, ASCENT, AXES, BACKPACK, BALANCE, BELAY,
BOOST, BOOTS, CARE, CLIFFS, CONDITIONS, CRAG, CRAMPONS,
EQUIPMENT, EVEREST, EXPEDITION, EXPLORE, FALL, FOOTHOLD, GEAR,
GLACIAL, GRIP, GUIDE, HAND, HIGH, HIKE, ICY, LEAD, LINE, OVER,
OXYGEN, PHOTOGRAPHY, PULL, RANGE, REACH, RESCUE, RISK,
ROPES, SCENERY, SKILL, SLOPES, SPIKES, STEEP, WEATHER, WINTER

158

New Orleans Food

Solution: 11 letters

B	E	A	N	S	E	K	O	H	C	I	T	R	A	C
G	A	R	L	I	C	G	O	O	D	J	E	C	I	R
H	C	N	E	R	F	I	U	T	A	B	A	S	C	O
B	A	R	C	S	O	S	T	M	E	A	L	S	R	Q
E	F	E	A	S	T	M	B	A	B	L	S	D	E	U
Q	P	H	S	I	N	A	P	S	M	O	T	B	O	E
E	C	I	P	S	L	Y	U	O	G	O	I	R	L	T
N	F	U	R	A	N	D	A	R	T	R	R	E	E	T
I	R	R	Y	T	O	O	I	I	A	P	G	A	P	E
S	U	A	E	O	Y	L	T	N	N	N	I	D	U	S
I	I	T	F	S	L	E	R	I	N	D	T	E	N	O
U	T	A	T	A	H	V	E	A	L	E	I	S	G	U
C	E	E	D	H	S	I	F	D	E	R	R	A	E	P
S	R	E	S	C	O	N	C	O	C	T	I	O	N	S
S	S	C	H	I	C	O	R	Y	X	I	M	M	T	S

AROMATIC, ARTICHOKES, BEANS, BREAD, CHICORY, CONCOCTIONS, CRAB, CREOLE, CROQUETTES, CUISINE, DINNER, FEAST, FRENCH, FRESH, FRUIT, GARLIC, GOOD, GRILLADES, GRITS, GUMBO, INDIANS, JAMBALAYA, MEALS, MIRLITON, MIX, OYSTERS, POTPIE, PUNGENT, REDFISH, RESTAURANTS, RICE, SEAFOOD, SOUPS, SPANISH, SPICE, TABASCO, TRIPE, VEAL, YAMS

159

Off to the Circus

R	V	E	I	R	W	O	H	S	R	E	G	I	T	S
S	E	S	N	N	R	A	T	S	D	O	V	E	S	M
T	T	D	W	T	A	S	U	N	R	A	C	E	A	A
E	R	O	I	I	E	M	S	O	A	N	E	R	N	E
N	L	A	D	R	F	R	A	E	A	H	C	Z	R	T
C	L	A	P	F	N	T	T	R	N	H	P	I	A	T
R	R	S	O	E	E	O	P	A	D	T	F	E	A	G
K	E	R	T	R	Z	R	I	I	I	B	A	L	L	L
P	U	N	O	P	E	E	U	L	S	N	E	E	F	E
M	O	P	I	L	U	C	K	L	S	N	M	A	R	E
S	E	L	G	A	L	F	A	N	T	T	N	E	I	G
S	E	G	E	H	R	M	T	L	I	T	R	N	N	A
S	U	A	O	V	I	T	B	R	A	V	E	E	G	T
J	E	S	T	N	E	T	T	S	A	F	E	C	S	S
O	T	F	A	M	I	L	Y	B	I	R	D	S	S	S

ANIMALS, BALL, BIRDS, BRAVE, CLAP, CLOWN, DARK, DOVES, DRAMA, ELEPHANT, ENTERTAINMENT, EVENT, FAMILY, FANTASY, FAST, FIRE, FLAG, FORUM, GAZE, GLEE, GREATNESS, HOST, JEST, JUGGLER, KNIVES, LEVEL, LION, LUCK, LURE, MARCH, NETS, PILES, POLE, PRANCE, RACE, RAIL, RIDER, RINGS, ROPES, SCENE, SEAT, SHOW, STAGE, STAR, STRESS, SWIFT, TALENT, TEAMS, TENT, TIGERS, TILT, TRAINER, TRAPEZE, TREK

Our Big Day

Solution: 11 letters

F	E	A	T	T	G	E	E	S	R	E	W	O	L	F
P	A	L	S	N	N	N	G	X	G	I	V	E	R	S
A	S	A	B	Y	A	P	I	R	C	P	N	S	R	K
C	O	E	P	A	A	S	A	D	O	I	N	G	I	S
T	H	P	I	R	R	D	A	S	R	O	T	D	S	W
E	A	R	T	R	U	O	H	E	I	A	S	I	E	E
H	N	I	I	A	A	P	M	T	L	D	W	D	N	N
S	E	J	T	S	M	S	A	E	R	P	D	E	T	G
S	G	I	O	U	T	R	R	A	M	I	S	L	R	N
T	O	N	I	Y	B	E	W	E	N	E	B	P	O	I
N	S	R	I	E	A	A	N	G	V	R	F	O	P	N
U	T	A	L	N	B	B	S	I	I	I	E	E	H	N
O	G	E	E	U	E	E	L	D	N	F	N	P	Y	I
M	C	M	S	F	E	P	E	E	N	G	T	N	U	W
A	S	Y	A	D	I	L	O	H	T	S	S	S	A	S

AMOUNTS, ANNIVERSARIES, AWARDS, BRIDE, BUSY, CELEBRATIONS, CHRISTENINGS, ENJOYABLE, EXCITING, FEAST, FEAT, FINE, FLOWERS, GIFTS, GIVERS, GRADUATION, HAPPY, HOLIDAYS, KIDS, LIVES, MEMORABLE, NEWS, OPENINGS, PALS, PARTIES, PEOPLE, PLEASANT, POSH, REWARDING, RINGS, RISE, SUPER, TOAST, TRIUMPHS, TROPHY, WEDDINGS, WINNING

161

Parenting

F	Y	L	L	I	K	S	U	P	P	O	R	T	E	H
A	A	T	T	I	R	E	S	D	I	K	S	I	G	U
M	D	T	I	E	V	R	E	Y	O	E	D	M	N	G
I	O	A	H	L	S	C	E	O	P	I	O	E	A	S
L	T	T	O	E	I	A	C	O	S	R	R	E	R	B
Y	O	V	H	S	R	B	H	C	A	A	C	E	R	I
M	N	S	I	S	E	S	I	L	C	I	G	E	A	T
I	I	O	T	L	A	P	L	S	F	A	A	S	L	S
W	N	A	I	F	L	V	D	I	N	D	N	U	G	D
S	K	E	E	I	A	G	R	E	W	O	C	I	N	R
E	F	T	N	L	U	C	E	I	I	I	P	S	I	A
S	Y	E	U	I	A	T	N	T	F	H	L	S	L	W
F	E	E	D	S	A	N	U	F	O	S	O	U	E	E
K	S	E	T	L	E	A	I	M	S	A	V	E	E	R
D	N	I	K	R	C	D	E	S	I	R	E	S	F	E

ARRANGE, BELIEFS, BREADWINNER, CARE, CAST, CAUTIONS, CHILDREN, COOK, DECISIONS, DESIRE, DIFFICULT, DISCIPLINE, FAMILY, FATHERS, FEED, FEELING, GUIDE, HOME, HOPES, HUGS, INVOLVE, ISSUES, KEEN, KIDS, KIND, LOVE, MORAL, MOTHERS, RESPONSIBILITY, REWARDS, SACRIFICE, SAFETY, SAVE, SKILL, STAKE, SUPPORT, TALK, TEENAGERS, TIME, TIRES, TODAY, VALUES, WISHES, YEARS

Phone Directories

Solution: 14 letters

D	E	M	S	S	C	O	M	P	A	N	I	E	S	A
I	T	U	T	S	E	T	A	D	R	E	L	E	Z	T
S	A	S	N	P	S	N	D	H	Z	I	C	O	N	A
T	T	T	E	E	S	R	O	I	S	N	N	E	B	P
R	S	E	M	C	E	R	S	H	E	E	I	T	R	D
I	Y	A	E	S	I	G	E	D	P	N	L	O	E	A
C	N	T	S	H	N	V	I	B	E	E	F	T	R	D
T	E	E	I	I	S	S	R	V	M	E	L	E	I	T
S	S	T	T	C	E	S	N	E	S	U	A	E	N	T
C	F	S	R	R	R	O	I	S	S	S	N	O	T	E
O	I	C	E	E	C	R	I	N	T	E	R	I	G	A
L	N	A	V	O	E	O	O	L	H	F	G	R	H	K
O	D	O	D	P	N	C	K	N	I	U	A	A	O	T
R	C	E	A	S	E	M	O	H	C	L	L	O	P	Y
S	S	P	E	C	I	F	F	O	K	L	L	A	M	S

ADDRESSES, ADVERTISEMENTS, AREAS, CITY, CODES, COLORS, COMPANIES, CONSULTED, CONVENIENT, COVERS, DATES, DISTRICTS, FIND, FRONT, HOMES, INK, LARGE, LISTINGS, LOOK, MUST, NAMES, NUMBERS, OFFICE, PAGES, PAPER, PRINTED, PROFESSIONS, READ, RESIDENCES, SERVICES, SHEETS, SIZE, SMALL, STATE, TELEPHONES, THICK, THIN, TITLES, USEFUL, ZONE

163

Plato

Solution: 12 letters

R	M	T	W	D	R	E	N	S	L	O	T	I	R	C
A	E	E	E	E	O	N	I	G	U	E	M	E	N	O
R	I	P	D	A	O	O	A	N	O	L	S	S	T	L
V	E	R	U	S	C	T	G	I	S	Y	E	W	A	Y
I	O	H	A	B	B	H	A	T	D	T	I	I	T	E
D	E	E	P	E	L	T	E	I	A	S	T	I	C	A
E	R	T	A	O	H	I	A	R	E	N	L	E	C	E
A	A	U	A	E	S	L	C	W	E	A	E	A	S	E
S	T	T	N	T	O	O	T	U	E	R	D	P	U	S
Y	A	I	H	G	S	H	L	R	G	E	V	O	R	U
K	A	I	U	E	O	F	L	I	M	D	I	L	D	C
N	E	E	T	U	N	A	I	Y	H	E	R	O	E	A
I	S	E	G	I	E	S	P	A	R	P	T	G	A	R
H	P	H	R	D	R	I	U	W	E	T	U	Y	H	Y
T	T	F	I	G	C	C	P	S	E	H	E	S	P	S

ACADEMY, APOLOGY, ATHENIAN, ATHENS, BEAUTY, CRITIAS, CRITO, DEPTH, DIALOGUES, GAIN, GIFT, GOOD, GREECE, GREEK, IDEAL, IDEAS, INFLUENTIAL, MENO, ORDER, PHAEDRUS, PHILOSOPHER, PUPIL, REALITY, REASON, REPUBLIC, SOCRATES, SOUL, STATE, STYLE, SWAY, SYRACUSE, TEACHER, THINK, THOUGHT, TONE, VIEW, VIRTUE, WISE, WRITINGS

Plumbers Are Needed

Solution: 8 letters

G	W	S	I	G	E	T	P	L	U	M	B	E	R	S
L	O	P	R	N	C	I	K	N	I	S	R	U	S	T
U	B	M	O	I	N	S	K	A	E	L	E	S	L	D
E	L	A	N	W	E	O	T	S	P	T	P	S	R	K
T	E	L	I	O	T	P	N	U	H	A	A	A	H	J
W	F	C	P	L	E	E	O	G	R	N	I	P	E	B
A	A	I	P	F	P	D	I	T	I	N	R	T	L	S
D	R	T	L	X	M	L	T	T	F	E	S	O	P	L
S	T	E	E	L	O	F	A	I	S	A	C	M	S	B
D	E	U	L	R	C	T	L	S	W	K	U	H	H	U
R	P	H	U	I	I	E	U	A	T	P	N	C	V	R
I	I	O	C	O	E	R	C	B	R	I	N	N	E	S
L	P	G	N	R	E	F	R	U	I	E	C	A	N	T
L	I	F	L	O	O	D	I	N	R	N	S	R	T	E
R	E	P	P	O	C	T	C	W	G	B	G	B	S	M

BLOCK, BRANCH, BULK, BURST, CIRCULATION, CLAMPS,
COMPETENCE, COPPER, CURB, DEPOSIT, DRAIN, DRILL, ELBOW,
EXPENSES, FILE, FLARES, FLOOD, FLOWING, GLUE, HELPS, IRON, JETS,
LEAKS, LIFT, LIGHT, NIPPLE, PIPE, PLASTIC, PLUMBERS, POUR, PRESSURE,
PUMPS, RELIEF, REPAIRS, RUST, SANITATION, SINK, STEEL, STEM,
TORCHES, TRAPS, TUBING, TURNS, VENTS, WADS, WASTE, WATER,
WRENCH

165

Raising Cash

Solution: 11 letters

E	F	F	O	R	T	S	G	S	P	U	O	R	G	C
V	R	U	I	M	C	O	O	K	I	E	S	B	O	A
E	E	A	N	A	O	G	G	S	I	N	C	O	F	U
N	T	N	R	D	N	S	L	A	O	A	K	O	A	S
T	T	E	W	I	R	I	T	I	N	I	O	K	D	E
S	E	I	B	A	A	A	T	D	N	D	I	S	S	S
P	L	C	A	M	P	A	I	G	N	S	R	B	E	T
L	L	Z	D	A	N	D	R	S	N	E	O	M	I	C
S	A	E	R	O	A	O	T	E	E	O	A	E	T	E
B	R	T	D	T	H	I	I	T	S	R	R	E	I	J
A	Y	E	E	G	U	T	N	T	A	E	S	T	R	O
K	R	S	N	R	E	U	E	T	C	A	A	H	A	R
I	A	E	C	N	L	S	H	M	L	U	A	R	H	P
N	V	E	P	O	I	O	T	E	L	L	A	B	C	O
G	R	N	V	O	N	D	S	E	L	F	F	A	R	H

AUCTION, BAKING, BALLET, BAZAARS, BINGOS, BOOKS, BOOST, CAMPAIGNS, CANDIDATES, CARE, CAUSES, CHARITIES, COOKIES, COOKING, DINNERS, DONATIONS, EFFORTS, EVENTS, FADS, FOOD, FUNDRAISERS, GOODWILL, GROUPS, HALL, LETTER, MAILS, MARATHON, MEET, METHOD, OPERA, PARTY, PATRON, PLEDGES, PROJECTS, RAFFLES, RECRUITS, RESEARCH, SALES, VARY, VOLUNTEERS

Read My Lips

Solution: 6 letters

K	D	E	P	P	A	H	C	M	A	P	I	N	K	T
L	K	L	G	R	A	S	P	E	A	N	I	I	C	T
A	S	T	R	E	T	C	H	I	I	K	S	A	I	E
T	A	S	T	E	T	U	R	H	S	S	T	N	L	E
C	D	I	P	M	O	U	T	H	L	N	I	I	Y	T
E	E	H	Y	Y	E	N	C	A	O	R	P	T	F	H
F	T	W	K	S	E	L	N	C	G	S	U	O	G	G
R	C	R	R	C	O	R	B	N	T	A	S	N	U	I
E	E	S	C	I	E	R	I	I	E	F	I	G	M	L
P	N	A	P	T	N	K	C	B	X	N	L	U	S	H
R	N	I	X	E	O	K	D	L	N	E	S	E	E	G
E	O	E	H	M	E	N	L	U	L	C	L	V	S	I
S	C	L	S	S	U	C	T	E	L	U	R	F	P	H
S	H	T	O	O	M	S	H	E	P	U	F	F	E	D
M	A	E	R	C	E	V	I	T	C	A	R	T	T	A

ACCENT, ATTRACTIVE, BEAUTY, CHAPPED, COLOR, CONNECTED, CONTACT, CREAM, CURVE, CUTE, EXTERNAL, FLESH, FLEXIBLE, FULL, GRASP, GRIN, GUMS, HIGHLIGHT, KISS, LICK, LIPSTICK, MOUTH, MUSCLE, PAIR, PERFECT, PERKY, PINK, PRESS, PUFFED, ROSY, ROUND, SHINE, SKIN, SMOKING, SMOOTH, SOFT, SPEECH, STEP, STRETCH, STUNNING, TALK, TASTE, TEETH, THIN, TONGUE, WHISTLE, WRINKLE

167

Remembering High School

Solution: 9 letters

B	O	A	R	D	M	T	R	R	R	Y	D	O	B	Y
E	O	T	D	S	A	E	N	E	O	U	T	U	U	D
L	L	O	E	L	G	S	H	E	K	T	L	A	S	U
L	O	O	K	A	D	N	P	T	D	C	U	E	E	T
E	O	T	N	N	C	A	A	R	N	U	O	T	S	S
E	C	E	E	O	A	H	N	G	I	A	T	L	S	K
P	E	I	U	N	A	P	E	C	M	V	A	S	R	N
T	R	R	L	O	G	S	R	E	I	A	O	T	S	
F	S	I	L	B	N	I	O	A	R	L	W	T	M	I
E	I	S	N	I	U	F	T	E	C	E	U	E	E	R
K	S	E	D	C	I	P	T	A	M	K	L	N	E	E
F	A	I	L	N	I	E	R	O	C	B	C	P	C	E
O	U	A	U	D	F	P	H	O	O	U	O	A	X	H
G	T	N	R	A	E	Y	A	R	M	R	D	A	R	C
E	S	O	C	I	A	L	P	L	T	I	M	E	E	T

ANTHEM, BELL, BOARD, BODY, BOOK, BUSES, CAFETERIA, CHEER, CLASS, CLUB, COOL, COURSE, DANCE, DESK, EDUCATION, EXAM, FAIL, FIELD, FRIENDS, GANGS, GUIDING, HALLS, HOMEWORK, KNAPSACK, LATE, LOCKER, LOOK, LUNCH, MEET, PRINCIPAL, PRIVATE, PROBLEMS, PROM, PUBLIC, REPORT, RULES, SEAT, SOCIAL, STUDENT, STUDY, TALK, TEACHER, TEENAGER, TIME, TRACK, TUTOR, UNIFORM, YEAR

Ribs, Ribs, and More Ribs

Solution: 6 letters

F	R	E	S	H	K	D	V	Y	R	O	K	C	I	H
C	A	O	D	N	E	R	C	I	S	L	I	S	T	E
C	R	R	V	M	O	U	O	D	N	L	E	E	E	T
T	H	I	M	A	M	I	F	P	R	E	V	C	E	I
G	O	I	S	I	L	I	T	A	O	A	G	U	W	U
N	R	T	N	P	R	F	G	A	C	N	T	A	S	Q
T	E	I	D	E	U	C	E	B	R	A	B	S	R	S
D	C	V	L	M	S	P	R	E	E	A	J	U	U	E
M	M	H	O	L	A	E	C	M	P	B	P	U	W	M
A	E	I	A	P	E	I	O	T	P	A	A	E	N	O
E	S	S	R	R	P	D	O	S	E	S	S	K	R	H
T	S	I	P	E	C	M	K	O	P	T	A	O	E	P
S	K	D	S	A	A	O	S	U	E	I	X	M	E	D
A	B	E	S	T	R	P	A	R	T	N	E	S	B	R
C	R	E	O	L	E	E	N	L	S	G	T	S	A	F

BAKED, BARBECUED, BASTING, BEER, BEST, CAJUN, CHARCOAL, CHINESE, COOKS, CREOLE, CRISP, CUMIN, FARM, FAST, FIRE, FLAVOR, FRESH, GARLIC, GRILLED, HICKORY, HOME, LEAN, LIST, MEAT, MESQUITE, MESS, MOIST, MUSTARD, OVEN, PAPRIKA, PART, PEPPERCORNS, PORK, PREPARATIONS, RECIPES, ROASTED, SAUCES, SIDE, SMOKE, SORT, SOUR, SPARE, SPREE, STEAM, STEP, SWEET, TEXAS, TOMATO, TRIMMED, VINEGAR, WESTERN

169

Rice Is Nice

S	E	M	C	P	L	E	H	T	U	O	S	M	H	S
T	N	O	R	A	S	E	G	A	W	A	T	E	R	R
C	F	L	O	O	D	I	N	G	V	D	A	D	O	E
E	U	D	P	S	W	H	I	T	E	T	L	I	U	Y
F	P	L	D	E	R	E	H	T	A	G	K	U	G	A
F	L	R	T	R	O	H	S	E	Z	I	S	M	H	L
E	M	O	O	I	I	E	E	G	S	D	L	E	I	F
H	L	U	U	D	V	P	R	O	C	E	S	S	E	D
P	U	R	T	R	U	A	H	S	O	O	G	N	M	P
B	L	L	A	A	N	C	T	E	E	O	R	G	E	A
R	L	H	L	A	T	E	E	E	O	I	R	Y	V	T
O	E	A	R	I	L	I	A	D	D	A	D	I	Z	N
W	S	I	C	O	N	O	O	I	I	L	T	D	A	A
N	E	L	I	K	E	G	N	N	S	A	I	R	A	L
S	I	V	O	R	Y	N	S	G	S	A	B	W	T	P

ASIA, BLACK, BRAN, BROWN, CROP, CULTIVATED, EFFECTS, FIELDS, FLOODING, FLOUR, GATHERED, GOOD, GRAINS, GRANARIES, HARVESTED, HEAT, HELP, HULLING, IVORY, LAYERS, LIKE, LONG, MEDIUM, MOLD, MUTATIONS, ORYZA, PADDIES, PATNA, PLANT, PLOT, PROCESSED, PRODUCED, ROUGH, SATIVA, SEEDING, SELL, SHORT, SIZES, SOAP, SOUTH, STALKS, THRESHING, VIOLET, WAGES, WATER, WHITE, WILD

Rockabye Baby

S	Y	S	A	S	E	E	E	S	C	D	S	B	S	H
T	L	O	T	U	E	G	L	R	E	R	R	I	G	U
N	I	S	L	N	A	L	Y	B	E	I	S	B	N	G
A	M	B	G	I	E	I	T	H	A	R	D	S	I	S
F	A	I	R	N	N	R	T	T	E	V	R	O	L	E
N	F	R	O	G	I	A	A	L	O	E	O	R	B	S
I	A	C	W	N	F	R	L	P	P	B	I	L	I	S
C	T	H	G	I	N	O	A	A	D	G	O	F	S	I
S	D	N	A	H	R	T	I	C	N	N	E	W	M	K
B	P	A	B	T	I	D	O	I	B	E	A	O	S	S
T	O	Y	S	E	T	P	S	F	D	L	T	R	C	T
O	W	Y	N	E	E	R	E	I	K	H	O	A	G	W
T	D	C	S	T	U	E	N	E	E	N	L	C	A	I
S	E	C	I	N	L	G	R	R	L	E	I	R	K	N
L	R	O	O	M	S	S	S	S	S	M	P	E	S

BIBS, BLOCKS, BLUE, BODIES, BOTTLES, BOWS, BOYS, CARING, CARRIAGE, COPE, CRIBS, CRYING, DIAPERS, FAMILY, FATHERS, FEEDINGS, FEEL, GIRLS, GRANDPARENTS, GROW, HANDS, HUGS, INFANTS, KISSES, LOVABLE, MOTHERS, NICE, NIGHT, NURSING, PACIFIERS, PATIENCE, PINK, POWDER, RITE, ROOM, SCALES, SIBLINGS, SLEEP, STROLLERS, TEETHING, TOTS, TOYS, TWINS, WALKERS, WARM

171

Romantic Moments

Solution: 10 letters

H	T	I	A	F	G	N	I	D	N	I	B	N	S	P
R	S	I	N	C	E	R	I	T	Y	D	O	B	U	N
A	E	W	B	O	N	D	I	N	G	I	C	L	S	O
G	R	L	E	A	F	F	E	C	T	I	O	N	T	I
N	E	C	A	E	T	A	R	A	D	Y	U	N	A	T
I	L	L	U	T	T	S	C	L	A	D	R	Y	I	A
R	A	O	T	A	I	I	A	L	T	A	T	T	N	R
A	X	S	Y	F	N	O	T	L	E	E	E	I	E	E
E	E	E	H	U	T	Y	N	Y	S	T	S	L	D	D
D	D	R	M	T	T	C	D	S	S	S	Y	I	S	I
N	S	M	R	S	R	E	E	R	H	I	O	B	T	S
E	O	U	E	E	N	O	U	P	E	I	A	A	A	N
C	S	N	A	S	D	E	W	L	S	A	P	T	B	O
T	O	L	U	F	G	N	I	N	A	E	M	S	L	C
H	C	A	R	I	N	G	L	A	D	V	R	T	E	E

AFFECTION, BEAUTY, BINDING, BODY, BONDING, CALL, CARING, CLOSER, COMMUNICATION, CONSIDERATION, COURTESY, DATES, DREAM, ENDEARING, FAITH, FATE, GLAD, HONESTY, LAST, LOYALTY, MEANINGFUL, RATE, REAL, RELATIONSHIP, RELAXED, RESPECT, SINCERITY, STABILITY, STABLE, STEADY, SUSTAINED, SWEET, TRUST, VALUE, WEDS, WORTH, YEARN

Scented Candles

Solution: 8 letters

M	O	O	R	H	T	A	B	S	T	I	C	K	P	E
S	U	N	F	L	O	W	E	R	T	S	B	O	O	K
R	A	L	L	I	P	L	H	A	N	D	L	D	U	A
N	O	E	B	T	L	S	D	J	I	E	O	V	R	W
O	M	F	R	E	S	H	V	E	M	R	W	A	O	A
S	E	G	N	A	R	O	T	O	R	T	K	N	W	X
E	L	H	R	L	T	R	N	J	A	S	M	I	N	E
S	O	G	O	I	E	I	Y	L	E	S	C	L	W	S
N	N	V	V	G	C	A	L	G	P	K	A	L	I	I
E	E	E	P	H	N	A	D	I	S	M	O	A	N	S
C	S	T	E	T	H	A	C	F	P	N	P	M	D	N
N	O	R	A	T	L	E	M	T	S	P	O	T	S	I
I	R	A	C	O	L	O	R	A	L	M	O	N	D	F
Y	T	T	H	B	A	S	K	E	T	E	M	A	L	F
G	T	C	E	L	L	O	C	I	N	N	A	M	O	N

ALMOND, APPLE, AWAKE, BASKET, BATHROOM, BLOW, BOOK,
CHERRY, CINNAMON, COLLECT, COLOR, FLAME, FRESH, GIFT, GRASS,
HALL, HAND, HOLDERS, INCENSE, JARS, JASMINE, KIWI, LAMP, LEAD,
LEMON, LOVE, MANGO, MELON, MELT, MULBERRY, NOSE, ODOR,
ORANGES, PEACH, PILLAR, POUR, SELL, SMELL, SMOKE, SNIFF, SORT,
SPEARMINT, SPICE, SPOT, STICK, SUNFLOWER, TALL, TART, TEA LIGHT,
VANILLA, VOTIVE, WAXES, WICKS, WIND

173

Seasonal Fashions

Solution: 10 letters

F	B	C	H	A	T	S	N	Y	T	G	S	E	I	T
R	I	E	O	E	E	O	D	R	A	C	E	L	L	C
A	E	T	L	T	I	N	O	B	A	B	R	P	R	H
L	S	A	S	T	E	U	D	R	O	E	C	E	A	I
L	P	S	A	R	S	N	F	R	T	O	M	E	S	C
O	O	E	T	E	A	L	D	A	M	M	T	T	S	L
C	R	C	R	H	O	R	E	F	U	O	Y	S	E	O
C	T	I	I	O	A	W	O	S	A	L	D	L	V	T
E	S	R	K	W	S	R	N	L	E	B	A	E	O	H
G	W	P	S	I	T	M	S	I	E	S	R	C	L	E
N	E	S	L	N	U	I	T	P	S	R	S	I	G	S
A	A	K	M	T	T	N	R	P	R	H	A	E	C	T
H	R	I	U	E	A	E	O	E	U	I	O	P	R	S
C	O	A	T	R	G	D	H	R	F	O	N	E	P	D
S	E	R	O	T	S	N	S	S	L	O	N	G	S	A

APPAREL, AUTUMN, BELTS, BOOTS, CAPE, CHANGE, CHIC, CLOTHES, COAT, COLLAR, COMFORT, CREATION, DENIM, DRESSES, FABRICS, FITS, FURS, GEMS, GLOVES, HANDBAG, HATS, HEEL, LONG, LOOK, MODELS, PALE, PRICES, SALE, SCARF, SETS, SHOES, SHORTS, SILK, SKIRT, SLIPPERS, SPORTSWEAR, SPRING, STORES, STYLE, SUMMER, SWEATER, TAGS, TIES, TRENDY, TROUSER, WARDROBE, WINTER

Shakespeare

Solution: 11 letters

E	Y	N	O	T	N	A	L	S	I	S	Y	A	L	P
R	E	T	I	R	W	O	E	D	R	A	H	C	I	R
C	A	E	S	A	R	I	C	Z	W	T	R	C	O	T
Y	R	N	E	H	D	I	L	A	A	O	K	M	S	T
N	O	V	A	E	F	A	H	L	B	S	E	I	U	R
A	A	B	M	I	S	T	E	E	I	O	T	L	C	A
R	E	O	L	T	A	T	S	D	E	A	I	T	I	G
T	C	O	S	H	S	U	R	N	M	O	M	E	N	E
A	R	S	U	I	N	E	G	A	T	E	S	C	O	D
P	R	L	L	E	J	L	R	L	T	E	M	U	R	I
O	O	Y	V	U	I	D	O	G	E	F	E	D	D	E
E	H	R	L	S	E	H	T	N	N	I	O	O	N	S
L	T	I	H	N	A	O	C	E	I	W	P	R	A	T
C	U	C	N	N	N	H	A	M	L	E	T	P	D	I
S	A	A	Y	E	L	S	E	H	T	O	I	R	W	W

ACTOR, ANDRONICUS, ANNE, ANTONY, AUTHOR, AVON, BACON, CAESAR, CLEOPATRA, COMEDIES, DRAMATIST, ENGLAND, ENGLISH, GATES, GENIUS, HAMLET, HATHAWAY, HENRY, JULIUS, LASTS, LINE, LIST, LYRIC, PICKS, PLAYS, POEMS, PRODUCE, PROLIFIC, RICHARD, ROBES, ROMEO, STRATFORD, TALE, TOIL, TONE, TRAGEDIES, VENUS, WIFE, WILLIAM, WIT, WRIOTHESLEY, WRITER

175

Shipwrecks of the Bronze Age

Solution: 12 letters

S	E	N	O	B	S	T	E	R	N	S	L	O	P	E
N	D	F	A	T	O	M	B	R	S	S	M	A	S	T
A	A	N	I	E	A	S	E	G	Y	P	T	I	O	O
I	R	N	I	L	N	G	S	A	R	T	O	O	L	G
B	C	V	T	F	A	A	B	E	I	O	N	I	A	N
U	H	A	L	L	R	L	R	T	A	A	U	S	T	I
N	E	A	M	D	N	F	U	R	E	I	G	G	O	S
W	S	T	I	I	O	A	I	A	E	T	A	G	T	P
K	E	N	N	V	L	S	N	D	D	T	R	F	F	E
R	I	R	E	O	A	E	T	U	A	I	A	A	E	
A	E	U	C	R	S	E	R	C	G	T	D	C	D	
N	B	T	Y	S	D	K	T	A	T	R	E	E	E	
O	A	R	M	A	A	E	L	E	E	H	E	E	S	M
S	O	C	L	A	Y	Y	D	O	B	R	C	A	A	I
Y	B	G	O	K	K	A	D	E	G	A	C	O	S	T

AKKO, AMBER, ARCHES, ASCALON, BAYS, BOAT, BODY, BONES, BURNT, CAGE, CARGO, CASE, CHARTS, CLAY, COST, CRETE, CREW, DATE, DEEP, EGYPT, FACE, FIND, FLAGS, FLASK, GIFTS, GLASS, GOAL, GOLD, GREAT, GREECE, INGOT, IONIAN, IVORY, LIFE, MALTA, MAST, MEDITERRANEAN, MINE, MYCENAEAN, NUBIAN, REGAL, RUIN, SARDINIA, SLOPE, SONAR, STERN, SYRIA, TIME, TOMB, TOOL, TRACE, TRADE, TROY, TURKEY, UGARIT

Sleigh Rides

Solution: 12 letters

T	Y	A	W	S	H	T	I	S	S	S	T	T	I	M
I	N	O	S	O	L	P	N	T	P	N	D	E	V	I
U	N	E	R	S	A	L	N	A	G	U	D	A	S	G
S	H	S	M	R	O	E	E	N	S	I	O	E	O	Y
E	E	I	T	I	D	C	I	B	S	A	I	R	L	R
S	R	I	G	U	R	G	I	Y	H	T	E	L	G	J
N	E	E	T	H	N	R	R	A	I	G	O	L	I	S
S	E	S	H	I	S	T	E	R	T	J	I	N	P	T
S	O	R	S	P	N	C	O	M	E	I	G	E	E	A
E	L	R	D	U	S	R	H	G	U	L	O	L	L	E
H	A	E	O	L	O	O	E	O	E	S	K	N	K	S
T	U	C	I	S	I	L	M	T	O	C	I	S	S	C
O	G	G	P	G	L	H	U	T	A	L	I	C	T	A
L	H	A	S	O	H	O	C	R	A	R	S	N	A	R
C	C	A	C	T	R	S	C	I	B	N	F	G	H	F

ASSOCIATIONS, ATMOSPHERE, BRISK, CAPS, CHILDREN, CLOTHES, COLLEGE, COUNTRYSIDE, CRACKLE, FRATERNITIES, GROUPS, HATS, HIGH SCHOOLS, HORSES, HUGS, JINGLE, JOLLY, LAUGH, MERRIMENT, MITTS, MUSIC, NICE, PARTIES, PLEASANT, ROADS, ROUTE, SCARF, SEATS, SINGING, SLEIGH BELLS, SLEIGHS, SNOW, SORORITIES, STUDENTS, SUIT, SWAY

177

Snails

Y	F	T	H	H	H	L	S	E	T	E	R	C	E	S
M	A	E	T	S	L	M	A	R	D	N	O	P	D	T
D	A	R	E	E	A	E	E	C	E	I	I	P	E	E
T	E	R	G	L	K	S	N	N	I	C	B	N	E	G
R	F	E	L	F	E	O	I	G	E	P	T	L	F	N
A	E	S	W	D	S	R	O	R	T	A	O	O	E	O
I	C	T	A	A	A	E	S	C	C	H	R	R	R	P
N	C	R	A	M	E	B	A	L	R	E	E	E	T	S
F	K	I	A	W	O	S	E	S	S	E	H	D	C	E
A	L	A	L	W	Y	S	M	T	O	T	E	L	I	K
L	I	L	L	I	L	K	O	W	I	N	E	P	L	H
L	S	S	S	A	Y	I	L	L	C	I	E	R	L
X	S	L	L	F	R	U	S	P	C	A	H	N	A	R
M	O	L	L	U	S	K	T	G	S	W	O	O	G	T
W	F	B	B	S	G	N	U	L	L	E	H	S	P	S

BOWL, BOX, BURY, CHOP, CILIA, COOK, CRAWL, CREEP, DARK, DESERT, EDIBLE, FEED, FEELERS, FLESH, FOREST, FOSSIL, FRESH, GARLIC, GRAY, HEAT, HIDE, HILL, LENGTH, LUNGS, MARINE, MOIST, MOLLUSK, OPEN, POND, RAINFALL, RECIPE, SEASONING, SEAWEED, SECRETE, SHELL, SLITHER, SLOW, SLUG, SMALL, SOIL, SPIKY, SPONGE, STEAM, SURF, TENTACLES, TERRESTRIAL, TROPICAL, WATER, WHELK, WINE

Soft Music

Solution: 11 letters

S	L	A	E	P	D	A	R	S	F	L	U	T	E	S
C	R	L	R	V	S	N	W	E	A	U	H	E	A	R
O	M	R	I	O	I	E	U	T	V	B	S	R	A	L
M	S	E	N	S	E	T	N	O	A	E	T	E	U	Y
P	I	G	L	T	T	E	A	L	R	S	R	F	S	R
O	S	N	N	O	M	E	L	E	E	G	T	I	E	I
S	T	I	D	I	D	A	N	H	R	H	K	V	E	C
E	I	S	T	R	D	I	C	J	G	C	O	C	E	S
R	R	N	E	S	T	R	E	U	O	L	F	L	A	O
S	E	A	E	Y	O	O	O	S	A	Y	T	L	I	B
S	M	S	E	N	R	H	N	C	P	N	A	D	O	D
S	A	Z	T	G	T	T	O	A	E	L	A	B	O	W
B	O	G	A	F	E	V	F	G	I	R	A	O	L	M
D	A	N	C	E	U	Y	N	O	H	P	M	Y	S	E
E	N	T	V	I	O	L	I	N	S	Z	T	L	A	W

BACKGROUND, BALLADS, BASE, COMPOSERS, CREATIVE, DANCE, DOZE, DREAMS, ENJOYABLE, FLOW, FLUTE, FUSES, GENTLE, HEAR, LISTEN, LOVE, LYRICS, MELODIES, MERIT, MIND, MOOD, ORCHESTRAS, ORGAN, PEALS, PIANO, PLAY, RADIO, RECORDINGS, RESTFUL, REVERIE, SENTIMENTAL, SERENITY, SINGER, SOFT, SONGS, SWEET, SYMPHONY, THOUGHTFUL, VIOLINS, VOCAL, WALTZ

179

Speaking of High School

E	K	C	O	J	D	D	W	G	R	A	D	E	S	R
N	S	S	U	R	S	O	L	O	S	F	R	C	O	E
S	A	E	A	T	R	O	I	N	U	J	O	O	G	F
P	T	M	S	K	M	N	B	T	P	H	M	D	R	I
O	A	E	H	K	E	A	U	U	A	S	A	E	E	R
R	T	S	A	S	F	R	T	R	L	S	N	A	E	M
T	A	T	L	E	E	E	D	H	S	C	C	N	T	C
S	E	E	L	D	A	R	A	O	H	A	E	I	H	P
D	S	R	S	C	R	P	F	T	M	T	N	E	I	L
C	N	P	H	D	S	T	H	R	S	K	M	S	L	I
L	O	E	A	L	A	B	O	Y	S	I	E	S	H	G
A	R	P	I	N	E	F	M	G	S	P	E	E	C	H
S	U	P	E	R	I	A	E	T	I	I	A	R	R	T
S	O	Y	N	N	F	S	R	A	Z	R	C	T	A	G
H	C	N	U	L	S	Y	H	N	E	L	L	S	M	D

BOYS, CHEMISTRY, CLASS, COPE, DARE, DEAN, DESK, DRAMA, FADS, FEARS, FEATS, FRENCH, FRESHMAN, FRIEND, FUTURE, GIRL, GLEE CLUB, GRADES, GREEK, GREET, HALLS, HARD, HEAR, HOME, INKS, JOCK, JUNIOR, LEARN, LUNCH, MARCH, MATH, MEANS, PALS, PENS, PEPPY, PHYSICS, PLIGHT, RIFE, ROMANCE, ROOMS, SEAT, SEMESTER, SENIOR, SIZE, SOFT, SOLOS, SPANISH, SPEECH, SPORTS, STRESS, SUPER, TASK, TEACHERS, TESTS, UNIFORM, WORK

Spending Spree

Solution: 7 letters

P	S	A	R	E	D	W	O	P	W	P	O	T	C	P
P	E	R	F	U	M	E	E	K	S	I	A	I	Y	A
T	A	D	O	L	L	T	C	O	Y	T	N	D	L	O
O	R	P	A	S	T	E	I	O	A	O	O	E	S	S
Y	E	H	E	E	S	S	R	B	R	O	R	R	I	M
S	S	D	S	R	B	I	P	T	P	A	E	C	E	T
M	N	S	I	A	O	B	C	M	S	P	T	M	N	F
S	A	I	C	V	W	E	A	S	A	S	B	I	A	I
C	E	T	P	O	L	H	S	T	E	L	A	S	O	G
G	L	O	V	E	S	P	T	N	H	P	T	L	S	N
W	C	O	H	D	J	M	E	U	E	R	T	E	G	O
A	R	L	T	S	R	E	E	N	O	B	E	B	U	I
T	E	S	N	H	D	E	W	T	S	M	R	A	M	T
C	A	N	D	L	E	T	S	E	I	O	Y	L	D	O
H	M	R	E	T	A	E	W	S	L	C	A	R	D	L

BATH, BATTERY, BOOK, BOWLS, CANDLE, CARD, CASSETTE, CLEANSER, CLOTH, COMB, COSMETIC, CREAM, CREDIT, DECORATION, DOLL, DRESS, ELECTRONIC, GAME, GIFT, GLASS, GLOVES, JEWEL, LABEL, LAMPS, LOTION, MIRROR, MOUTHWASH, MUGS, NEEDLE, OILS, PADS, PAINT, PAPER, PASTE, PENS, PERFUME, PINS, POWDER, PRICE, SALE, SCISSORS, SHOES, SOAP, SPRAY, STORE, SWEATER, SWEETS, TAPE, THREAD, TOOLS, TOYS, VIDEO, WATCH, WINE

181

Sunday Dinners

Solution: 12 letters

L	S	N	H	N	E	H	S	A	W	T	S	E	U	G
A	E	D	O	O	F	T	F	D	F	E	E	B	R	S
U	T	I	S	I	V	K	A	I	N	R	H	T	E	O
G	S	M	T	T	T	I	M	S	E	S	V	H	N
H	A	E	O	A	E	A	E	S	I	H	I	A	T	E
G	T	A	G	S	G	T	R	K	S	T	D	R	A	R
N	D	T	V	R	P	E	A	E	A	O	N	Y	F	D
I	T	R	O	E	A	H	S	L	N	M	U	I	S	L
N	S	U	I	V	E	B	E	H	P	E	C	P	D	I
E	P	E	C	N	R	R	M	R	T	H	G	I	N	H
V	O	M	E	O	K	R	A	H	E	M	E	R	O	C
E	U	O	T	C	S	O	G	R	N	T	R	U	B	H
E	S	H	S	I	S	A	I	Y	R	T	S	A	P	A
R	E	N	N	I	D	S	C	H	E	E	R	I	W	R
R	S	G	U	H	H	T	L	A	I	C	E	P	S	M

ATMOSPHERE, BEEF, BONDS, BROTHER, CHARM, CHEER, CHERISH, CHILDREN, CONVERSATION, DATE, DINNER, DISHES, DRINK, EVENING, FATHER, FISH, FOOD, FRIENDS, GAMES, GENERATION, GROUP, GUEST, HOME, HOST, HOUSE, HUGS, INTIMATE, KISS, LAUGH, MAKE, MEAT, MOTHER, NIGHT, PASTRY, PLATE, REAP, RELATIVES, ROAST, SING, SISTER, SOUP, SPECIAL, SPOUSE, TASTES, VARY, VISIT, VOICE, WARMTH, WASH

182

Tasty Croissants

E	G	O	L	D	E	N	Y	S	H	M	N	D	A	P
C	C	O	E	F	E	S	T	T	L	C	E	E	L	P
R	H	I	O	G	T	L	S	Y	S	L	N	A	P	D
O	E	I	O	D	G	A	I	K	E	A	I	E	T	O
T	B	T	C	H	F	S	S	C	C	N	T	F	R	O
A	A	R	T	K	C	A	T	T	I	A	O	T	E	F
M	K	P	A	U	E	A	R	U	E	O	N	H	T	A
O	E	E	E	S	B	N	A	E	F	E	U	S	T	E
T	R	N	P	L	P	T	W	F	C	F	L	S	A	S
B	I	O	E	I	S	B	B	S	I	L	I	N	L	E
A	E	I	P	S	A	F	E	M	O	L	U	N	P	E
N	S	N	P	P	U	R	R	R	A	T	L	F	G	H
A	Z	O	E	L	C	I	R	E	R	P	P	I	H	C
N	V	A	R	I	E	T	Y	N	S	Y	L	N	N	G
A	B	E	S	T	S	L	E	M	A	H	C	E	B	G

BAKERIES, BANANA, BECHAMEL, BEST, BREAKFAST, BUTTER, CHEESE, CHICKEN, CHIP, CHOICE, CRESCENT, DELECTABLE, DELICIOUS, EGGS, FARE, FEST, FILLING, FILLS, FINE, FRENCH, FRESH, GOLDEN, GOOD, HONEY, MAPLE, MEAT, ONION, OPEN, PEPPERS, PLAIN, PLATTER, RASPBERRY, ROLLS, SAUCES, SEAFOOD, SNACKS, SPLIT, STRAWBERRY, STUFFING, TASTE, TASTY, TOMATO, TUNA, VARIETY

183

The Color Is Orange

Solution: 8 letters

S	E	U	H	E	N	I	R	E	G	N	A	T	C	S
Y	P	P	O	E	E	O	F	L	A	M	E	U	C	K
A	E	K	U	C	A	R	M	L	E	E	P	R	C	H
R	E	N	N	O	U	T	H	M	O	S	E	I	I	C
P	H	I	E	I	L	S	O	Y	I	W	P	E	T	R
N	R	T	T	I	A	Y	C	D	S	E	O	R	O	
P	I	A	O	F	O	L	T	R	I	N	R	R	U	T
O	P	K	D	M	S	R	I	N	R	R	A	E	S	R
M	N	L	P	D	A	V	A	P	A	E	P	R	P	U
G	O	P	A	M	E	T	R	C	S	C	B	A	B	S
G	R	S	L	R	U	H	O	O	H	T	I	O	Q	T
L	F	O	S	U	O	P	C	E	V	C	I	U	W	T
O	F	I	V	O	P	C	E	P	S	A	A	C	S	L
W	A	C	R	E	L	S	N	I	L	S	L	E	K	I
E	S	O	R	E	E	B	T	R	H	E	Z	F	P	W

APRICOT, BERRY, BLOSSOM, BOWL, BRANDY, CANTALOUPE, CAROTENE, CARROT, CENT, CHEDDAR, CHEESE, CITRUS, CORAL, CUPS, FIRE, FLAME, FLAVOR, FLOWERS, FRUIT, GLOW, GOLDFISH, GROVE, HEAT, HUES, LIPSTICK, MOTH, PEACH, PEEL, PEKOE, PERSIMMON, PICK, PRINCE, PULP, PUMPKIN, RAYS, RIPE, ROSE, RUST, SAFFRON, SCREWDRIVER, SQUASH, TANGERINE, TOMATOES, TORCH, TREE, WILT, ZEST

The Diamond Industry

Solution: 6 letters

D	E	M	A	N	D	U	R	A	B	L	E	E	C
A	T	L	A	I	R	T	S	U	D	N	I	T	W	S
S	R	R	R	A	E	S	E	G	C	I	G	N	A
A	N	O	A	F	K	S	V	A	S	L	O	O	H	W
S	C	O	R	N	E	E	G	I	R	R	I	L	H	T
K	T	I	I	L	S	E	T	E	S	S	U	O	O	E
A	C	N	W	T	M	P	B	I	U	A	L	O	X	R
A	F	A	E	E	C	M	O	L	N	E	R	P	B	I
Q	L	F	N	M	I	E	C	R	S	G	E	B	G	A
F	U	T	L	K	T	N	F	A	T	N	L	E	A	T
R	S	A	O	U	I	S	L	R	S	A	O	A	H	I
A	O	O	L	C	E	E	E	I	E	L	B	G	V	L
E	L	U	E	I	R	N	V	V	O	P	I	L	A	O
L	T	S	G	S	T	E	C	G	N	E	M	E	E	S
C	E	T	I	H	W	Y	Y	E	W	I	R	I	N	G

ABRASIVE, AFFLUENCE, AFRICA, AWE, BOURSES, CLEAR, COLOR, DEMAND, DURABLE, ENGAGEMENTS, EXPENSIVE, FLAWLESS, GEOLOGY, IMPERFECTIONS, INCLUSIONS, INDUSTRIAL, INVESTMENTS, KIMBERLITE, LIGHT, LOOK, MARKETING, NICE, OVAL, QUALITY, REAL, RING, ROCK, ROUGH, SOLITAIRE, TRANSPORTABLE, WEIGHT, WHITE, WHOLESALERS

185

The Gift of Talent

S	T	U	D	Y	T	N	E	M	G	D	U	J	G	S
L	E	V	E	L	S	V	A	L	U	E	D	N	E	Y
S	E	G	N	I	H	C	A	E	T	E	I	L	T	G
W	S	A	A	C	A	I	M	S	D	N	L	S	N	O
S	I	E	R	T	T	N	I	I	I	I	E	I	E	C
V	S	S	N	N	S	N	C	A	N	N	T	V	I	D
P	I	E	E	E	C	A	R	G	O	C	I	S	I	A
R	P	T	N	E	T	T	M	H	A	T	U	S	C	W
E	O	T	R	I	T	U	L	B	C	M	C	O	W	A
P	L	E	O	C	S	I	T	E	I	I	S	U	R	R
A	I	N	E	G	V	U	P	S	P	T	T	T	I	E
R	T	R	F	I	O	S	B	L	A	R	I	L	T	N
E	I	A	N	E	R	A	I	I	U	G	W	O	I	E
D	C	G	L	E	E	N	L	T	O	N	E	O	N	S
T	S	S	P	K	E	L	H	S	W	O	R	K	G	S

ACTING, AIMS, AMBITION, ASTUTENESS, AWARENESS, BUSINESS, DEDICATION, DIRECT, DISCIPLINE, FACT, FEEL, GOALS, HONESTY, JUDGMENT, LEARN, LEVELS, LIVING, MUSIC, OUTLOOK, PERSPECTIVE, POLITICS, POTENTIAL, PREPARED, SAGE, SELLING, SINCERE, STAGE, STUDY, TALK, TEACHING, TRAINING, TRUTH, VALUE, WISE, WITS, WORK, WRITING

The Last Days of Summer

Solution: 10 letters

I	N	E	H	L	E	D	C	S	N	G	I	S	S	R
V	R	E	N	A	A	S	R	H	N	C	Y	I	E	O
S	G	E	T	D	R	T	E	I	A	T	H	T	V	L
S	N	N	H	A	I	V	N	P	V	N	F	I	I	O
C	E	W	I	T	M	N	E	E	T	E	G	A	L	C
G	U	R	A	R	A	I	G	S	M	E	P	I	L	L
E	N	S	U	L	O	E	L	A	T	I	M	O	N	L
G	K	I	P	T	T	T	W	C	C	I	T	B	G	G
S	N	I	L	A	A	A	S	K	H	H	N	N	E	L
C	M	I	B	O	R	R	L	R	I	A	I	G	E	R
D	A	L	L	D	O	I	E	N	E	N	N	A	E	S
U	E	M	R	O	N	H	G	P	E	M	V	G	E	Y
S	T	O	P	G	O	O	C	P	M	E	R	E	E	K
K	B	S	B	U	L	C	I	S	S	E	R	A	C	S
E	B	R	E	D	S	R	A	C	T	T	T	L	F	E

BIKE, CAMPUS, CARES, CARS, CHANGES, CHANGING, CHILL, CITY, CLIMATE, CLOTHING, CLUBS, COLOR, COOLING, CUSP, DRIVE, DUSK, ENDING, FALL, FARMERS, GOLD, HARVESTING, LAWNS, LEAVES, LIVES, PICKLING, PLANNING, REDS, REGRET, RIPENING, SCHOOLING, SENTIMENTAL, SEPTEMBER, SIGNS, SKY, STORING, TASKS, TEAM, TEMPERATURES, TREES, VEGETABLES, WARDROBE, WEATHER

187

The Mayan People

M	H	E	H	C	E	P	M	A	C	E	P	M	D	R
A	O	C	A	N	C	I	E	N	T	A	A	F	E	I
P	O	N	S	I	R	A	H	A	L	T	S	O	H	S
S	R	A	T	T	T	I	L	A	H	T	T	R	S	D
A	A	I	P	Z	N	E	C	E	N	E	R	E	I	I
P	N	L	E	A	S	E	M	E	N	A	R	S	R	M
A	A	L	C	S	S	A	M	O	C	D	C	T	U	A
I	T	I	N	T	T	U	H	E	Y	O	A	S	O	R
H	N	R	O	I	N	S	N	N	V	B	G	R	L	Y
C	I	B	C	O	P	T	A	E	A	E	N	A	F	P
W	U	S	M	U	U	S	R	S	R	V	I	V	I	D
R	Q	O	O	R	T	I	C	L	U	I	D	H	I	A
I	A	R	I	I	E	O	G	L	I	L	A	A	C	Y
T	G	E	E	S	O	Y	M	O	N	O	R	T	S	A
E	S	S	E	K	L	O	S	T	S	I	T	R	A	M

ACHIEVEMENTS, ANCIENT, ARTISTS, ASTRONOMY, BRILLIANCE, CALENDAR, CAMPECHE, CENTURIES, CHIAPAS, CONCEPT, COOK, DISCOVERIES, DRESS, DYNASTIES, FLOURISHED, FORESTS, GROUPS, HALT, ITZA, LIVE, LOST, MAPS, MATHEMATICS, MAYA, MOAT, MONUMENTS, PALACES, PAST, PRIESTS, PYRAMIDS, QUINTANA ROO, RACE, RAID, RICE, RUINS, SHONE, TABASCO, TALES, TOLL, TRADING, VIVID, WRITE

The SAT Test

Solution: 8 letters

P	L	L	A	H	S	H	T	A	M	P	A	S	S	S
N	O	T	E	S	L	S	Q	S	Y	T	S	E	T	T
P	O	H	K	P	E	G	U	I	D	E	M	G	A	U
Y	T	I	S	R	E	V	I	N	U	I	A	A	N	D
S	L	S	T	K	P	N	Z	G	T	P	R	U	D	E
L	K	T	H	S	R	H	S	R	S	E	C	G	A	N
E	R	O	C	S	E	O	Y	W	T	N	T	N	R	T
S	M	R	O	F	H	U	W	G	R	C	X	A	D	C
E	T	Y	L	B	C	R	Q	R	O	I	E	L	I	S
D	N	R	L	Y	A	S	S	E	P	L	T	G	O	C
M	A	X	E	S	E	N	C	A	E	S	O	T	T	I
D	L	T	G	S	T	F	S	D	R	L	O	I	E	E
N	P	E	E	R	S	A	R	W	N	I	A	R	B	N
I	S	S	U	B	M	I	T	C	E	J	B	U	S	C
M	U	L	T	I	P	L	E	E	T	R	A	I	N	E

ANSWER, BIOLOGY, BOOKS, BRAIN, COLLEGE, CRAM, DATE, ESSAY, EXAM, FAIL, FORMS, GRIDS, GUESS, GUIDE, HALL, HISTORY, HOME, HOURS, LANGUAGE, LOGIC, MATH, MIND, MULTIPLE, NOTES, PASS, PEERS, PENCILS, PENS, PLAN, QUESTION, QUIZ, READ, REPORT, REST, SCIENCE, SCORE, SKILL, SLEEP, STANDARD, STATE, STRESS, STUDENT, STUDY, SUBJECT, SUBMIT, TEACHER, TEST, TEXT, TRAIN, UNIVERSITY, WORKSHOP, WRITTEN

189

The Vegan Way

Solution: 13 letters

S	S	S	Y	R	E	L	E	C	S	S	V	E	G	S
E	R	N	T	S	U	S	D	O	P	T	L	E	S	H
T	C	I	I	N	M	D	A	I	E	S	D	S	O
S	T	A	C	A	A	A	S	A	T	E	U	I	L	P
A	E	H	R	E	R	R	E	T	L	B	D	U	E	S
T	E	L	T	R	A	G	U	B	U	A	F	A	N	S
S	G	S	O	B	O	C	A	A	R	O	S	A	T	N
T	R	I	M	R	E	T	T	A	T	R	R	S	I	E
M	E	A	T	L	E	S	S	C	L	S	A	P	L	H
M	E	N	U	G	A	S	H	I	O	F	E	I	S	C
N	N	A	E	P	A	O	S	N	K	O	A	R	O	T
O	S	V	L	S	P	I	N	A	C	H	K	L	E	I
I	S	E	H	S	I	D	E	G	C	N	O	I	F	K
N	D	I	N	N	E	R	S	R	I	R	D	F	N	A
O	S	H	E	R	B	I	V	O	R	E	S	E	M	G

ALFALFA, BARS, BEANS, BEETS, BREAKFASTS, BUDS, CARROTS, CASSEROLES, CELERY, CHOPS, COLOR, COOKING, DIET, DINNERS, DISHES, GRAINS, GREENS, HERBIVORES, KITCHENS, LENTILS, LETTUCE, LIFE, LUNCHES, MEALS, MEATLESS, MENU, ONION, ORGANIC, PASTA, PEAS, PODS, RADISH, RESTAURANTS, RICE, SALAD, SHOPS, SPAS, SPINACH, SPROUTS, STEAM, TASTES, TIPS, TOFU, TRIM, VEGETABLES

The World of Props

Solution: 9 letters

S	Y	T	I	L	A	E	R	E	T	R	A	P	S	S
I	R	H	C	H	A	I	R	S	T	N	H	R	M	O
C	R	E	A	T	I	V	E	U	S	O	E	O	N	I
L	P	A	S	P	M	A	L	O	T	N	V	L	V	D
O	E	T	T	I	T	E	L	O	T	I	S	E	A	U
T	R	E	S	S	T	U	G	A	E	M	N	E	D	T
H	I	R	F	J	T	R	L	S	R	A	S	R	L	S
I	O	S	U	I	A	S	E	I	M	G	T	P	U	L
N	D	G	O	P	Y	P	F	V	E	I	C	O	F	F
G	S	N	H	S	L	N	S	S	D	N	A	R	P	A
T	S	E	T	A	M	E	A	N	I	A	R	D	L	C
A	R	O	Y	O	G	V	T	P	C	T	T	K	E	T
S	C	S	L	A	C	I	S	U	M	I	N	C	H	I
K	O	D	T	T	A	B	L	E	S	O	O	A	R	N
S	S	S	T	R	E	C	N	O	C	N	C	B	Y	G

ACTING, ADVERTISERS, BACKDROP, CASTS, CHAIRS, CLOTHING, COMPANY, CONCERTS, CONTRACTS, CREATIVE, DEVOTE, FEEL, FIRMS, FURNITURE, HELPFUL, IMAGINATION, JUGS, LAMPS, MEDIC, MOLDS, MOVIES, MUSICALS, PERIODS, PHOTOGRAPHERS, PLAYS, REALITY, RENTALS, SEATS, SELL, SOLUTIONS, STAGES, STOCK, STUDIOS, TABLES, TALENT, TASKS, THEATERS, TRAPS, VASE

191

Those Final Exams

Solution: 13 letters

A	N	P	A	P	E	R	S	C	W	Y	M	W	S	O
C	H	I	R	O	P	R	A	C	T	O	R	S	T	C
H	R	E	G	U	E	S	S	I	O	I	R	E	U	O
E	S	A	M	H	L	A	S	R	T	S	N	R	D	U
S	G	U	M	O	T	R	N	I	O	G	S	N	Y	R
C	L	N	O	A	E	O	N	I	I	T	T	A	E	S
L	T	H	I	V	N	G	W	N	M	S	C	O	P	E
D	C	E	I	T	R	X	E	L	G	A	E	O	N	S
S	E	N	A	T	U	E	I	L	D	N	T	L	D	E
B	U	G	O	C	R	P	N	E	L	T	I	S	T	U
A	O	N	R	S	H	A	M	B	T	O	H	R	H	G
R	R	O	O	E	S	I	D	O	T	Y	C	A	I	I
T	A	T	K	T	E	E	N	E	C	A	R	B	N	T
S	T	L	U	S	E	R	L	G	S	D	A	I	K	A
L	A	W	Y	E	R	O	N	T	O	L	L	I	A	F

ACADEMIES, ACHES, ANXIETY, ARCHITECTS, ARTS, BELL, BOOKS, BRACE, CHIROPRACTORS, COLLEGE, COMPUTING, COURSES, CRAM, DEGREE, DOCTORS, ENGINEERS, FAIL, FATIGUE, GUESS, HARD, LAWYER, LESSON, MULL, NERVOUS, NIGHT OWL, NOTE, PAPERS, PASS, PRESS, RESULTS, ROOM, SCHOOLS, SCOPE, STAMINA, STUDY, TEACHING, THINK, TIRING, TOIL, TOLL, TRADES, UNIVERSITY, WORRY, WRITING

Tile It!

Solution: 6 letters

A	E	R	A	F	F	I	N	I	S	H	O	W	E	T
E	C	O	S	T	L	G	S	T	E	P	M	R	N	S
R	M	E	R	E	I	O	O	S	O	O	U	A	P	S
U	I	I	M	S	P	C	O	E	O	T	L	R	L	S
S	M	N	E	E	K	A	R	R	X	A	E	I	M	L
A	A	D	S	T	N	I	H	E	E	A	A	O	D	D
E	T	D	E	T	H	T	T	S	D	N	O	E	O	R
M	I	T	O	C	A	R	R	C	I	R	L	E	O	I
S	D	N	O	B	O	L	E	A	H	G	O	L	W	L
T	Y	N	O	C	E	R	L	S	N	E	O	B	A	L
R	S	X	O	W	A	E	A	A	H	C	N	R	T	W
E	E	H	O	M	C	R	T	T	O	E	A	U	E
S	S	R	I	R	A	C	R	O	E	I	L	M	O	Z
N	T	C	O	N	E	I	O	E	R	O	O	D	R	I
I	A	P	I	R	Y	L	D	C	T	A	E	N	G	S

ADOBE, AREA, BATHROOM, BOND, BORDER, BOXES, CEMENT, CERAMIC, COLOR, COST, DECORATE, DESIGN, DIAMOND, DOOR, DRILL, ENTRANCE, FINISH, FLOOR, GROUT, INSERTS, INSTALLATION, KITCHEN, MALL, MARBLE, MEASURE, NAILS, NEAT, PORCELAIN, RECTANGLE, REST, ROOMS, SEALANT, SHAPES, SHINY, SHOW, SIZE, SPREAD, STEP, STOCK, TERRA COTTA, TEXTURE, THRESHOLD, TIDY, TOOL, TRIM, TROWEL, WALL, WOOD

193

Tinkering with Old Cars

F	R	E	T	R	E	K	C	A	T	E	L	S	S	F
I	S	I	U	V	L	U	C	G	U	I	T	E	R	E
B	R	S	R	A	T	I	N	L	A	R	V	A	P	B
E	T	A	T	T	I	G	T	O	R	M	A	U	K	O
R	C	E	I	S	D	T	E	N	U	E	T	M	O	O
G	M	N	A	L	T	D	G	C	R	F	P	O	R	A
L	G	L	E	M	O	R	H	C	R	E	L	L	I	F
A	P	W	E	I	T	D	A	P	R	N	N	I	C	E
S	E	O	U	S	T	R	E	P	I	D	T	T	N	M
S	D	R	Q	O	P	A	T	C	H	E	S	L	P	E
K	G	K	I	L	H	D	P	I	A	R	C	A	O	L
C	E	S	T	I	T	N	I	A	P	F	N	E	O	B
A	S	A	N	D	P	A	P	E	R	E	R	N	S	O
R	O	G	A	P	S	T	O	O	L	S	G	U	N	R
C	E	H	O	L	E	S	S	S	R	O	O	D	S	P

ANTIQUE, BOLT, BUMPER, CARVE, CHROME, CRACKS, CURVES, CUTTING, DETAIL, DOORS, EDGES, FENDER, FIBERGLASS, FILLER, FRAME, GAPS, GLUE, HINGE, HOLES, LINE, LONG, LOOK, METAL, NICE, PAINT, PANELS, PARTS, PATCHES, PATIENCE, PIECES, PLASTIC, PROBLEM, RENT, RUST, SANDPAPER, SOLID, STANDARD, STRONG, SURFACE, TACK, TAPE, TIRE, TOOLS, WELDING, WORKS

Tonight Is Chinese

B	S	D	U	M	P	L	I	N	G	S	Y	R	C	N
U	H	C	R	E	G	N	I	G	S	R	A	O	A	A
D	H	T	H	N	E	S	T	Q	D	G	E	I	H	W
S	M	O	O	R	H	S	U	M	E	E	L	E	O	C
P	C	F	I	R	Y	A	E	N	L	O	L	N	N	C
A	S	H	I	S	B	S	I	C	G	W	T	I	O	S
R	S	M	E	S	I	V	A	N	I	O	E	R	O	D
E	P	D	A	S	H	N	O	N	N	R	N	A	D	B
R	R	U	N	L	T	M	E	C	T	S	L	D	L	E
I	O	C	K	O	C	N	A	S	T	H	O	N	E	A
B	U	K	N	O	M	B	U	A	O	O	E	A	S	N
S	T	E	G	T	B	L	R	T	B	U	I	M	O	S
S	S	N	O	A	O	C	A	M	S	N	P	L	U	M
E	U	O	G	S	H	N	A	W	H	C	E	Z	S	M
Y	R	E	L	E	C	B	T	A	E	M	B	A	R	C

ALMOND, BAMBOO, BEANS, BOILED, BOK, BROTH, BUDS, CABBAGE, CANTONESE, CELERY, CHESTNUTS, CHOY, CHRYSANTHEMUM, CLAMS, CORNSTARCH, CRABMEAT, DORE, DUCK, DUMPLINGS, FISH, GINGER, GREENS, HOISIN, MANDARIN, MELON, MONGOLIAN, MUSHROOMS, NEST, NOODLES, PLUM, RICE, ROOT, SOUP, SPARERIBS, SPROUTS, SQUABS, SZECHWAN, VINEGAR, WINE, WONTON, YES, YUNG

195

Travel Consultants

Solution: 11 letters

S	S	S	O	F	F	I	C	E	S	S	E	C	O	S
R	E	E	S	E	U	R	O	P	E	C	M	S	P	E
O	L	L	E	R	U	M	S	N	I	F	N	U	G	S
O	G	U	L	I	E	E	A	V	A	O	O	A	N	T
M	N	D	S	S	G	L	R	R	I	R	Y	O	A	R
S	I	E	I	A	P	E	E	T	G	O	I	B	S	I
T	S	H	K	I	S	S	O	V	V	T	S	S	T	P
R	A	C	C	O	M	M	O	D	A	T	I	O	N	S
O	A	S	S	S	O	S	E	N	R	R	A	T	E	E
P	A	W	A	R	E	A	I	U	M	S	T	T	I	L
R	X	I	P	A	L	T	S	T	N	O	E	I	L	B
I	S	A	S	S	T	A	I	E	K	T	I	C	U
A	H	O	T	E	L	S	A	T	C	S	B	E	O	O
N	N	A	D	V	E	R	T	I	S	I	N	G	L	D
S	E	L	B	A	T	S	T	R	O	S	E	R	S	S

ACCOMMODATIONS, ADVERTISING, AIRPORTS, ASIA, AWARE, BILL, CLIENTS, CRUISES, DEALS, DESTINATIONS, DOUBLES, EUROPE, FARES, GROUPS, HOTELS, ISLES, MOTELS, OFFICES, PACKAGES, PLANES, PROMOTIONS, RATE, RESORTS, ROOMS, SCHEDULES, SEASONS, SELLS, SERVICE, SINGLES, SITES, STATES, TABLES, TABS, TAX, TICKET, TRAINS, TRAVELERS, TRIPS, TRUST, VOYAGE

True Love

Solution: 8 letters

N	I	O	J	O	Y	L	P	L	E	N	I	D	K	D
T	B	O	N	D	O	R	A	L	A	E	R	E	A	D
R	R	M	N	Y	E	N	I	I	T	A	E	N	N	M
T	E	A	A	V	R	M	I	N	C	P	C	O	E	G
S	C	L	E	E	S	K	E	D	S	E	M	O	N	S
R	R	R	T	H	R	M	I	A	E	A	P	I	C	G
I	O	E	A	E	T	D	K	S	I	A	D	S	S	U
F	N	R	W	I	R	E	O	D	S	D	L	G	N	H
S	E	T	M	O	R	U	E	E	E	H	N	I	S	S
I	E	M	I	U	L	S	S	W	C	O	O	R	Z	S
N	O	T	T	M	O	F	A	Y	S	N	E	L	O	E
C	O	U	A	P	A	L	F	L	M	T	A	T	D	R
U	F	T	O	D	K	T	E	W	T	B	F	M	U	A
S	E	R	E	S	H	C	E	E	P	S	O	I	O	C
S	P	S	E	S	O	R	L	N	G	N	O	L	G	R

BOND, CANDY, CARD, CARESS, COMMITMENT, CUTE, DANCE, DATES, DIAMOND, DINE, DREAM, ETERNAL, FEEL, FIRST, FLOWERS, FOREVER, FUTURE, GIFT, HOLD, HUGS, IDEALIZE, INTIMATE, JOIN, JOY, KEEPSAKE, KISS, LETTERS, LONG, LOYAL, NEWLYWEDS, NOTES, POEM, PROPOSE, REAL, ROMANCE, ROSES, SHARE, SMILE, SONGS, SOUL MATES, SPECIAL, SPEECH, SURE, SWEETHEART, SYMBOL, UNION, WALKS, WEDDING

197

Western Festivals

Solution: 5 letters

R	M	U	S	I	C	A	M	P	F	I	R	E	O	L
O	S	R	S	R	O	T	A	T	C	E	P	S	S	A
P	H	D	S	R	B	A	R	R	E	L	S	N	D	U
E	X	C	I	T	I	N	G	A	A	A	A	M	R	N
M	S	D	N	K	N	C	O	D	L	C	I	P	E	N
A	E	R	S	A	O	A	R	I	K	S	I	G	H	A
G	A	W	O	S	R	S	P	T	S	E	T	N	O	C
B	O	B	T	H	E	X	H	I	B	I	T	I	G	S
C	O	U	N	T	R	Y	O	O	C	T	H	P	R	D
E	M	L	A	E	M	N	C	N	W	I	A	O	O	U
E	D	L	H	S	L	A	N	I	F	V	T	R	T	A
V	R	A	C	O	M	P	E	T	E	I	S	R	R	L
E	A	A	R	P	S	O	N	G	S	T	A	E	A	P
N	W	D	E	A	E	N	O	I	E	C	N	A	D	P
T	A	R	M	G	P	Y	V	S	T	A	E	S	E	A

ACTIVITIES, ADMISSION, ANNUAL, APPLAUD, ARENA, AWARD, BARN, BARRELS, BULL, CAMPER, CAMPFIRE, CART, CLAP, COMPETE, CONTEST, COSTUME, COUNTRY, COWS, DANCE, EVENT, EXCITING, EXHIBIT, FINALS, GAME, GEAR, HATS, HERD, HORSE, KIDS, LASSO, MEAL, MERCHANT, MUSIC, PARADE, PARTICIPANTS, PONY, PROGRAM, RACING, RANCH, RIDE, ROPE, ROPING, SEATS, SHOW, SNACK, SONGS, SPECTATORS, TRADE, TRADITION, VISITORS

Windows

Solution: 8 letters

R	V	G	A	R	A	G	E	I	M	S	Y	A	B	S
W	E	A	T	H	E	R	E	X	I	T	C	A	R	S
M	N	F	C	B	O	W	S	E	R	E	L	R	O	E
O	E	A	L	N	L	E	O	L	T	L	O	R	K	S
B	T	A	I	E	O	R	D	P	S	B	S	I	E	I
S	I	B	S	P	C	A	E	U	H	A	E	A	N	R
G	A	R	E	U	K	T	N	G	P	R	L	P	Y	N
C	N	N	D	N	R	S	I	E	E	U	L	E	R	U
A	S	I	A	S	E	E	A	O	E	D	S	R	I	S
H	L	R	N	T	N	K	T	E	N	H	I	L	A	R
S	C	E	N	R	I	N	S	T	A	L	L	L	S	D
E	C	I	F	F	O	U	W	D	P	I	I	A	S	R
R	T	U	M	T	O	M	E	S	T	O	R	M	A	A
F	L	I	G	H	T	M	I	S	T	S	O	U	L	Y
S	I	G	N	I	R	E	V	O	C	L	E	D	G	E

AIRY, BAYS, BIRDS, BOWS, BROKEN, CABIN, CARS, CATS, CLOSE, COVERING, CRANK, DURABLE, EXIT, FRESH, GARAGE, GLASS, HOUSE, INSTALL, LEDGE, LEFT, LIGHT, LOCK, MALL, MEASURE, MIST, MORNING, NEIGHBOR, OFFICE, OPEN, PANE, PEAK, PLEXI, POWER, REFLECTION, REPAIR, SEAL, SHADE, SIGN, SLIDE, SOUL, STAINED, STARE, STILL, STORM, SUNRISE, SUNSET, TINT, TRIM, VENETIANS, VIEW, WEATHER, YARD

199

You Have to Have Heart

B	S	L	S	S	Y	T	I	N	A	M	U	H	P	G
S	H	Y	A	E	P	O	C	T	R	A	M	S	R	N
E	C	T	A	T	N	I	E	C	I	R	P	U	I	I
L	U	I	S	W	N	S	H	N	C	I	E	C	O	T
A	M	L	H	I	L	E	E	S	H	V	T	C	R	S
I	F	A	T	T	N	A	M	S	D	H	O	E	I	A
C	E	R	R	Y	E	C	N	I	G	N	A	S	T	L
R	E	O	U	R	P	O	E	I	T	L	E	S	Y	B
E	L	M	E	D	I	P	R	R	O	N	E	I	U	L
M	I	E	O	T	R	A	A	E	I	B	E	S	R	N
M	N	O	A	I	S	C	G	H	N	T	I	S	V	F
O	G	L	M	T	T	T	S	E	T	N	Y	C	A	I
C	E	A	U	S	L	A	E	D	E	S	I	W	L	R
R	R	T	B	R	A	I	N	S	H	S	I	W	U	S
Y	E	L	A	I	R	T	S	U	D	N	I	E	E	T

ALWAYS, ASTUTE, BEST, BRAINS, BUSINESS, COMMERCIAL,
CONTRACTS, COPE, DEALS, ETHICS, FEELING, FIRST, FRIENDSHIPS,
GOOD, HAPPY, HUMANITY, INDUSTRIAL, LASTING, MARRIAGE,
MORALITY, MUCH, PRICE, PRIMARY, PRIORITY, REAL, RELATIONSHIPS,
RICH, RIGHT, SENSES, SENTIMENTAL, SINCERITY, SMART, SUCCESS,
TEST, TRUE, VALUE, WINNER, WISE, WISH

Yummy Chocolate

Solution: 8 letters

A	B	T	H	G	I	L	E	S	S	E	C	O	R	P
M	E	C	U	A	S	T	R	F	U	O	M	C	M	F
E	I	S	H	A	R	D	A	I	G	T	E	O	E	O
R	E	D	W	O	P	T	Y	N	A	E	T	L	L	N
I	O	M	T	E	S	W	I	E	R	F	S	O	T	D
C	F	U	D	G	E	K	R	F	O	P	U	R	E	U
A	W	F	Q	H	L	T	S	S	I	W	S	R	G	E
N	M	F	C	I	R	A	R	H	B	C	W	O	N	R
D	U	I	M	U	L	S	C	A	S	A	I	V	I	U
E	I	N	F	N	D	T	K	P	C	N	R	A	L	T
S	G	F	N	N	S	Y	R	E	A	D	L	S	L	X
S	L	L	A	B	H	E	A	F	K	Y	O	E	I	E
E	E	R	E	Y	A	L	D	O	E	L	E	E	F	T
R	B	I	B	D	K	E	S	O	I	C	I	N	G	T
T	W	H	I	T	E	K	I	D	S	M	O	O	T	H

AMERICAN, ARTIFICIAL, BALL, BARS, BEAN, BELGIUM, BRAND, CAKE, CANDY, CART, CHEWY, CHIPS, COLOR, DARK, DESSERT, FATS, FEEL, FILLING, FINE, FONDUE, FOOD, FREE, FUDGE, HARD, ICING, KIDS, LAYER, LEFT, LIGHT, LIQUOR, MELT, MILK, MOLD, MUFFIN, POWDER, PROCESS, PURE, RICH, SAUCE, SAVOR, SHAKE, SHAPE, SMOOTH, SOFT, SOLID, SPREAD, SUGAR, SWEET, SWIRL, SWISS, TASTY, TEXTURE, TORTE, TREAT, TRUFFLE, WHITE

WORD ROUNDUP
CHALLENGE

How to Play

Find the hidden words in the puzzle looking
horizontally, vertically, and diagonally.
Unlike traditional word searches, Word Roundup™
Challenge gives clues to the words hidden within
the puzzles. The words themselves are for
solvers to figure out.

201

```
K E L L E R M O L E C
X H L U L L A B Y X H
Z Y D E C A Y Y A Z R
S M Z E D X R V N Z I
U N U N X U J O T D S
B K A S T C Z C H A T
M P K N I X E A E L O
U X E L O C A L M L P
L C F O C U S Z X A H
O M E L O D Y J V B E
C H E L E N T U N E R
```

Find and Circle

Six words for "song"	○○○○○○
Five five-letter words with "C" in the middle ("uncle," for example)	○○○○○
Explorer who made a famous 1492 expedition (first/last name)	○○
Author who became blind and deaf when she was 1 (first/last name)	○○
100-year time period	○
Rock ____ or ____ box	○
Black-and-white bearlike mammal	○
Mammal, spy, or skin spot	○

```
S T A L P S F O A P X
E J O Z A L S A R U E
A C K M U G C K B D K
Z H O G Z D O Y E D A
R A V C N Y T O Z L L
E N Y O E S I Z N E E
T N P J E A A O I Q S
T E J Z X Z N N R A I
U L Z I L C H E A R U
B H A R B O R S N I R
J N O V A N S A L T C
```

Find and Circle

Nine bodies of water	○○○○○○○○○
Four five-letter words that begin with "Z"	○○○○
Rain Man star whose real last name is Mapother (first/last name)	○○
Two things commonly added to popcorn	○○
Two country neighbors with similar names	○○
Canadian province: ____ ____	○○
European mountain chain	○
Tree that produces acorns	○

203

```
S  M  E  L  T  C  E  N  T  E  R
X  B  Z  V  K  V  Y  E  M  Z  K
H  K  U  R  Z  D  Z  A  A  Y  L
Z  E  A  T  W  Z  M  S  D  O  I
V  H  L  O  T  A  Z  T  O  G  M
S  J  H  L  E  E  Z  E  N  U  X
G  T  F  R  O  J  R  R  N  R  H
U  U  C  M  A  T  H  N  A  T  C
A  O  C  E  N  T  R  A  L  T  R
R  R  C  H  E  E  S  E  Z  O  E
D  T  F  O  R  W  A  R  D  M  P
```

Find and Circle

Five dairy products	⃝⃝⃝⃝⃝
Four five-letter fish	⃝⃝⃝⃝
Three basketball positions	⃝⃝⃝
Two U.S. time zones	⃝⃝
Two five-letter words that mean "hi"	⃝⃝
Famous pop singer ____ Louise Ciccone	⃝
Algebra or calculus	⃝
Sawyer or Brokaw	⃝

```
C L E A R H Z X Y F R
F H U S K Y U Z K I A
Z O R A Y H S M M E I
Y K G V Z O E X I L N
D A X G I C V C T D Y
N A H D Y K O H T Z J
I L A O Y E L A E A H
W P Z N O Y G R N N O
Z S N H O L A L S D U
X U R O C K I E S E N
S B O X E R C S B S D
```

Find and Circle

Six five-letter weather conditions   ○○○○○○

Three mountain chains   ○○○

Three five-letter dog types   ○○○

Two things worn on the hands   ○○

Team sport in which players attempt to score goals by hitting the ball across the pitch with a stick (two words)   ○○

American blues pianist and singer (first/last name)   ○○

Spanish hello and goodbye   ○○

Popular site co-founded by Jerry Yang   ○

205

```
Z  W  I  N  F  R  E  Y  Z  X  Z
L  O  C  L  E  O  P  A  R  D  A
I  P  J  H  N  A  R  A  D  D  M
O  R  A  R  E  E  S  R  J  E  U
N  A  O  F  H  E  A  I  P  Z  P
N  H  F  T  R  G  T  O  A  R  Z
T  E  N  R  U  I  R  A  R  A  M
B  A  C  O  A  U  C  E  H  U  A
P  X  C  K  E  N  G  A  K  G  U
K  A  U  A  I  I  C  Z  Z  A  I
L  Y  N  X  T  O  A  H  U  J  X
```

Find and Circle

Nine felines	OOOOOOOOO
Three continents	OOO
Three Hawaiian islands	OOO
Popular host born in Mississippi in 1954 (first/last name)	OO
Former French currency	O
Sharp projection found on a rose stem	O
Head supporter	O
Combine to form a sum	O

206

```
S  H  E  R  D  P  F  L  O  C  K
W  T  P  Z  B  J  E  Z  J  P  C
A  T  O  O  K  E  X  N  N  A  O
R  I  E  M  N  B  N  R  N  C  L
M  M  C  P  A  T  U  N  Z  K  O
P  B  U  O  K  T  I  I  Y  B  N
O  A  T  T  A  X  O  A  C  X  Y
O  C  T  S  H  I  L  L  C  K  Z
R  O  E  C  A  D  I  L  L  A  C
T  N  L  S  E  A  N  B  U  L  L
P  O  D  X  Z  S  C  H  O  O  L
```

Find and Circle

Eight animal groups	OOOOOOOO
Four General Motors divisions	OOOO
BLT components	OOO
Risque English comedian who died in 1992 (first/last name)	OO
Ex-husband to Madonna (first/last name)	OO
Male bovine	O
The opposite of bottom	O
McGraw, Conway, or Burton	O

207

```
Y P O S E I D O N R T
G T F I V E R Y O X E
O X R D Z E C T T E C
L S E A P Z A F W N H
O R M P N N V I E U N
N O E I I S E F N T I
H P N M T P C Z T P C
C K R E Z H U R Y E I
E E W I L L Z M I N A
T S A L T T E N A B N
T E L E S C O P I C E
```

Find and Circle

Five 10-letter words that begin with "T"	OOOOO
Common denominations of U.S. paper money	OOOOO
Roman and Greek sea gods	OO
Two things that come in shakers	OO
Hancock and *I Am Legend* star (first/last name)	OO
Shoe brand, or cat	O
Natural underground chamber	O
Moscow's ____ Square	O

```
S O D A E H O W D Y P
J Z G E H E A R S E E
B E R L Y K E J R J E
U T E X E L Z L E E L
S B K P P A E G W W K
E L Y P K W S O O E Z
V O A C O N G O M L E
O S S T A I R S N C C
R S J A C K I E I Z A
G O F E W E R U K Y R
Z M V A N Z J T A X I
```

Find and Circle

Orange ____	○○○○○○
Six types of automobiles	○○○○○○
Five five-letter words with "W" in the middle ("tower," for example)	○○○○○
Actor who played Ralph Kramden (first/last name)	○○
Flight of steps	○
Granny Smith or McIntosh	○
Large waterfowl	○
Long African river also known as the Zaire	○

209

```
B B R U S S E L S C B
E B A R M S T R O N G
I R S B C O L L I N S
R A C P O O D L E T B
U S E Y K G N Z T S J
T I N Z Z I O X O E M
D L E B L U E T E P K
N I T R O G E N A A T
A A E A L D R I N D F
H B B E I J I N G U Z
B E R N C R I M E B X
```

Find and Circle

Eight country capitals that start with "B" ○○○○○○○○

Three *Apollo 11* astronauts ○○○

CSI: ____ ____ *Investigation* ○○

Colorless, odorless gas that constitutes
   about four-fifths of the atmosphere ○

Dog breed developed as a water retriever ○

Place for a glove ○

Type of crab or whale ○

Terminal digit of the human foot ○

210

```
C  C  Z  M  U  E  S  L  I  X  V
H  E  H  V  J  K  R  H  I  N  E
E  N  L  E  V  O  L  G  A  P  S
X  T  E  T  E  J  K  S  R  I  E
T  N  T  H  K  R  E  Z  B  C  E
H  O  T  O  Z  I  I  X  E  K  H
A  I  U  R  T  X  J  O  Z  L  C
M  N  C  A  P  O  N  G  S  E  T
E  O  E  L  I  N  C  O  L  N  R
S  H  D  A  N  U  B  E  J  Z  I
W  L  I  F  E  R  H  O  N  E  X
```

Find and Circle

Six cereal brands	○○○○○○
Five European rivers (five-letter minimum)	○○○○○
Four things that can go on a Whopper	○○○○
Sixteenth U.S. president	○
Black-and-white horselike mammal	○
Mythical god of thunder	○
Fast-paced sport: Ping-____	○
U.S. penny	○

211

```
T  M  O  N  G  O  L  I  A  T  N
S  D  J  Z  S  X  N  F  Z  S  E
I  J  E  G  V  A  F  R  A  I  U
R  P  U  N  M  K  O  E  I  R  R
T  B  O  R  T  C  N  S  T  O
E  Z  E  L  I  I  U  C  Y  A  L
M  G  J  X  I  J  S  H  A  I  O
O  M  E  R  V  S  Z  T  L  D  G
T  M  U  N  I  C  H  Z  A  O  I
P  T  O  W  E  L  J  X  M  P  S
O  O  N  C  O  L  O  G  I  S  T
```

Find and Circle

Five doctors	OOOOO
Three countries that start with "M"	OOO
Three six-letter European languages	OOO
The capital of Bavaria	O
Riddle: What gets wetter the more it dries?	O
Ford model with a vision-related name	O
____ Bunny	O
Wheel of Fortune creator ____ Griffin	O

```
P O V C O R I O L E V
A S A X A C O N D O R
L P L F Z N O U N V K
E R V P A R A G U A Y
T E E O P L Y R Z C K
O Y W A A E L J Y U N
R T E E K Z K S K U O
R L L R V I V I D M C
A P U R E V I V E Z L
P T P U F F I N Z J A
C O N T I N U U M X F
```

Find and Circle

Eight six-letter birds	OOOOOOOO
Three words that contain two "V"s	OOO
Three words formed from A-E-L-P	OOO
Two words that contain two "U"s	OO
A country with three "A"s in its name	O
Niagara _____	O
Person, place, or thing	O
Square root of four	O

213

```
K X B Z Y V G N R H F
H F Z L K Z N E E O R
C K O C U W O T T R I
N Y A O O E L F S S E
I L Z R T X R L U E N
B M B Z J R U I B Z D
D I Z J E X F X K E S
R L X D P I T T C G B
A E I M E T E R O I R
Y P D E A T H Z L E A
S F I N D E R S B B B D
```

Find and Circle

Six units of length	○○○○○○
Four colors that start with "B"	○○○○
Two competing movie rental companies	○○
Two words formed from D-E-F-I-N-R-S	○○
The Curious Case of Benjamin Button star (first/last name)	○○
Type of arachnid	○
Mammal with an Arabian breed	○
U.S. low spot: ____ Valley	○

214

```
L M U N I C H A U N T
U E A T R O P I C G X
O V I T C Z W J L N J
E E S Z H G Z A S I A
S R A Y I E E K Y J T
W E A P D R N X S I N
O S C X T N V S T E A
C T N N J Z E Z E B L
S Z O B U C K Y M Z T
X M C O L U M B I A A
M B A R C E L O N A Z
```

Find and Circle

Eight cities that have hosted the Olympics	OOOOOOOO
CBS: ____ Broadcasting ____	OO
Two three-letter farm mammals	OO
Sir ____ Newton	O
Earth's highest point: Mount ____	O
____ of Capricorn	O
Male deer	O
Your mother's or father's sister	O

215

```
E R I E T E A M C A P
H S U P E R I O R U M
U Z R C O A C H W N I
R X E G B A T J E I C
O O Y L L J Z S S F H
N I A A K O E V T O I
G R L K Z M V R E R G
A A P E A X C E R M A
M T F I E L D H N Y N
E N S V O L T A I R E
J O P E R S I A N P Z
```

Find and Circle

Baseball ____   OOOOOOOOO

The five Great Lakes   OOOOO

Two seven-letter cat breeds   OO

French philosopher, historian, satirist,
    dramatist, and essayist   O

A hemisphere   O

____ Seinfeld   O

Great Salt ____   O

Potato or poker, e.g.   O

```
M U S H R O O M S K Q
T U B A N I C K E L U
D R A C U L A O P Y E
A C B P Z S I V E X B
T L O C E R A K P Z E
R Y T K A N Z G P S C
E D I T Z N N K E N H
B E N A L L O Y R O E
L O A D I M E E S I E
A J M B O N N I E N S
N U N A V U T R Z O E
```

Find and Circle

Five Canadian provinces and territories	○○○○○
Five common pizza toppings	○○○○○
Three U.S. coins	○○○
Criminal partners Parker and Barrow	○○
Vampire created by Bram Stoker	○
Brass, for example	○
Anagram of "ocean"	○
Valved brass instrument with a low range	○

217

G R I M E T W O A E Z
D I M E H S I X L R K
S M I M E O E J F A R
R E I G H T U Z R E A
E T J Z U L M R E P H
K E X N E A Z Z D S S
C N I B I P O L O E T
I M O L F O U R L K I
N N L C H I M E I A M
S I T H Y M E Z M H E
W P R I M E J X E S Z

Find and Circle

Eight words that rhyme with "rhyme" ○○○○○○○○

Five even numbers ○○○○○

English playwright and poet (first/last name) ○○

Two clock hands ○○

Swedish inventor of dynamite who founded
  prestigious prizes with his fortune (first/last name) ○○

Candy bar introduced in the 1930s ○

Great white ____ ○

Response to "Marco!" ○

```
I  S  A  L  M  O  N  X  G  U  D
N  Y  M  Z  M  O  Z  N  C  N  E
E  T  Z  O  N  O  I  J  O  D  T
V  I  P  A  N  R  N  T  U  E  A
I  S  C  A  R  T  N  E  N  L  U
T  O  X  E  U  O  R  V  T  I  U
A  I  H  Y  R  L  K  E  Y  A  M
B  R  Z  O  L  A  R  V  A  B  U
L  U  T  M  U  L  L  E  T  L  C
E  C  C  A  L  G  A  R  Y  E  C
V  A  N  C  O  U  V  E  R  Z  A
```

Find and Circle

Four five-syllable words	○○○○
Four large Canadian cities	○○○○
Three fish (six-letter minimum)	○○○
It has a seat	○
Code of laws established by a church council	○
French painter Claude	○
Immature, wingless, feeding stage of an insect	○
____ Bunyan	○

219

D	U	B	L	I	N	Z	Z	E	M	E
X	M	B	E	I	R	U	T	I	A	K
Z	J	O	J	A	C	K	X	N	D	O
P	A	J	S	F	I	S	H	S	R	J
L	V	U	Y	C	S	X	Y	T	I	O
A	A	L	B	N	O	K	E	E	D	T
T	Z	Y	E	O	V	W	G	I	J	T
O	J	H	J	O	L	T	N	N	P	A
X	T	J	U	R	Y	T	A	N	E	W
A	L	I	S	B	O	N	R	E	E	A
H	A	V	A	N	A	Z	O	P	J	X

Find and Circle

Eight six-letter country capitals   ○○○○○○○○

Seven four-letter words that begin with "J"   ○○○○○○○

Albert ____   ○

Citrus fruit or color   ○

Greek philosopher   ○

Shark or eel, for example   ○

Lightning flash or a length of fabric   ○

Writing instrument that uses ink   ○

```
D D O C E A N M O L E
O E L A W R E N C E A
V E R T E B R A T E S
E R X A L Z L X Y Z T
W N Y O U Y I W Z D E
O O Z G M Z Z A X A R
L I X Y Z X A Y Y V N
F L Z P R Z R N Z I M
B S Y U A Z D E X D O
A E X M E Y S Z Y X S
Y A M A B B R U C E T
```

Find and Circle

Eight four-letter mammals	○○○○○○○○
Three bodies of water	○○○
Two 11-letter words	○○
Word Roundup creator Hoyt (first/middle name)	○○
Batman's alter ego (first/last name)	○○
Geckos and iguanas	○
Sweet potato	○
Chocolate brand, or certain bird	○

221

```
P A N T S G K C F B S
W A T C H R L E A N K
C Z S K O Z E O A B I
S D O P I B Y E V Z R
A I L J X N J I Y E T
G U I Z A T G V R G X
S Q D Q R C Y O T A F
S I Z I U A K R L T R
E L H V D E Z Y U E A
R S B I L L E J O S C
D P A R K A Z N P J S
```

Find and Circle

Nine five-letter things you wear	OOOOOOOOO
Three types of meat	OOO
Three forms of matter	OOO
Three playing cards	OOO
Wealthy Microsoft founder (first/last name)	OO
Tusk material or soap brand	O
Taxi	O
24-hour time period	O

222

```
Y P A A F E R I G O R
R H C G O C B O O A B
T Y E O R N H J L M I
S S O N T E Z U X A O
I I G Y U I G Z N N L
M C N K N N L I N G O
E S I Z A E I C E O G
H J B T T V I G O R Y
C Z C X E N D I N G O
D E V E L O P M E N T
R T O M Y C V I R G O
```

Find and Circle

Eight five-letter words that contain "GO" ○○○○○○○○

Four 11-letter words ○○○○

Three school subjects ○○○

Newscaster Connie ○

Selleck or Hanks ○

Startling three-letter exclamation ○

Card that can count as one or 11 in blackjack ○

Frozen H₂O ○

223

```
Y K C Z M Y P I G Y E
Y E Z E K O T R L Z T
L X S C N E U R Z Y I
L F U T M T A S M D H
U Y U L E E E M E R W
F J E M Y R U R E E P
H H E G B Y D Y K L O
T K Z R O L A A A K I
U V J X S L E Z Y C N
O B O B P E F K A A T
Y S A F E T Y J K T S
```

Find and Circle

Eight six-letter words related to football   ○○○○○○○○

Five words that start and end with "Y"   ○○○○○

Colors of Japan's flag   ○○

Mickey, Minnie, or Mighty ____   ○

Five-letter palindromic boat   ○

Sport with birdies   ○

____ Newhart   ○

Porky ____   ○

```
C A N D Y Y X W A L L
X C J R B V C X E W B
B D O U O I J L R A O
A R R N S B B V E X T
N I N U C B I G V L T
D V M E A E N N E O O
S E V R U I R K R B M
A K C J W T K T S S O
L S J S T O R K E T P
T B A T M A N A Z E A
  G A R D E N Z K L R L
```

Find and Circle

Rock ____	○○○○○○○○○
Three transmission options	○○○
The Dynamic Duo	○○
Two four-letter birthstones	○○
Hasbro crossword game	○
Bird associated with babies	○
Plane or bird feature	○
Candle material	○

225

```
M E O W I N G D I M E
B O J B K N K Z K V R
S R B Z E R I Y K E Z
N C X R O T N N D X R
O H H W E N W W E R E
W A T E E W O E E C T
M R J P W H E S E O R
A D A K C I W R V N A
N A M E N O N K Y E U
C H E E R I O G X Z Q
X Z S B S E A W E E D
```

Find and Circle

Nine seven-letter words with
  "W" in the middle   OOOOOOOOO

Three U.S. coins   OOO

Apple grove   O

British goodbye   O

Author Henry ____   O

The square root of 81   O

Waffle or sugar ____   O

Prayer ending   O

```
C O L O R K I T A L Y
A M B U L A N C E B K
Y V P O L A N D V Z E
R E A N C H O V Y N N
U N K Y T E S R R K E
C U Z R C R E U S N D
R S A E A T T U U I R
E E E M I A N T D A Y
M R Z P S A P Z O P E
G J U C R E E K G S R
K J K U N B R U S H B
```

Find and Circle

Eight planets	○○○○○○○○
Four European countries	○○○○
Hair ____ (five-letter answers)	○○○
Nine-letter emergency vehicle	○
Boxers and hounds	○
Small, herringlike fish	○
Brook	○
Boyfriend to Barbie	○

227

```
R A D I S H N Z E S C
C B R E P O R T M Q Z
P A Z C S E K Z A U Y
A R S R A O P A L A R
P R A U T R N P F S R
A O X A B A R K E H E
Y W M J N W J O Z R H
A O C A K E A Z T X C
T Z B T R I C Y C L E
C L Y D E H A R L E M
O R A N G E S M O K E
```

Find and Circle

Nine six-letter fruits and vegetables ⭕⭕⭕⭕⭕⭕⭕⭕⭕

Three five-letter words related to fire ⭕⭕⭕

Bonnie Parker's partner in crime (first/last name) ⭕⭕

Bike with three wheels ⭕

Northern Manhattan neighborhood ⭕

Underground rail system ⭕

____ card ⭕

Wedding or birthday ____ ⭕

```
A  L  E  O  S  U  N  S  E  T  L
R  G  J  P  K  V  O  K  T  X  I
I  X  E  Z  I  G  Z  E  C  S  B
E  C  X  M  R  S  S  V  I  T  R
S  F  O  I  I  C  O  R  A  A
S  L  V  L  R  N  I  E  T  R  X
U  O  M  N  U  P  I  R  S  R  O
R  W  U  I  R  M  X  E  I  R  G
U  S  J  O  L  K  B  P  D  U  N
A  Z  C  C  R  E  D  I  T  O  I
T  S  A  S  I  A  S  Z  A  H  R
```

Find and Circle

Eight zodiac signs	○○○○○○○○
What "mph" stands for	○○○
What "D.C." stands for	○○
Daylight beginning and end	○○
Beatles drummer (first/last name)	○○
Extra ____ (student's incentive)	○
Home to billions of people	○
Four-letter wild canine	○

229

```
S H O M E R J B V P Z
C P Z K J U L E S O D
O Z O Z N K L Y K O L
A V J O R I X I G C E
C E E O N A F N O H I
H R F L M Z I E V N F
C N Y A B M K N E E E
A E L K M O V I E V Z
T L J E C O W B O Y S
C X L E M U R L Z X G
H P I T C H G L Y N X
```

Find and Circle

Six five-letter words related to baseball	○○○○○○
Five mammals starting with "L"	○○○○○
Three eating utensils	○○○
20,000 Leagues Under the Sea author	○○
Two joints	○○
Hat-wearing horse-riders	○
Motion picture	○
Five-letter word for "dog"	○

230

```
Z M Y H E R B E R T Z
J A A E D Y I T O P P
M A N R L A S R R X I
Z U N U C U I E A R L
J L J U G H B S E N U
E I T U A O R B Y I T
G L A U T R M A M X L
R A I C R E Y A V I Z
O C O R V K L X R E J
E X Y O A A E P E N N
G K N Z S Q A Y H A M
```

Find and Circle

Nine months	○○○○○○○○○
Three deli meats	○○○
Three five-letter flowering plants	○○○
What H. G. Wells's initials stand for	○○
Two neighboring countries with similar names	○○
Bird with lustrous black plumage and a loud, harsh call	○
Writing instrument that comes in a fountain or ballpoint form	○
Highest point	○

231

```
S  A  L  T  C  J  H  O  T  E  L
P  R  E  D  I  C  T  A  B  L  E
X  B  P  A  N  I  C  N  O  B  C
E  I  G  X  J  W  W  E  L  A  G
L  T  N  Y  I  A  A  H  L  T  N
B  R  I  D  M  L  I  P  E  N  I
O  A  V  W  B  D  T  E  H  U  N
W  T  I  O  E  O  I  T  Z  O  I
C  I  L  H  N  K  N  S  X  C  D
C  O  N  T  I  N  G  E  N  C  Y
B  N  Z  H  O  S  P  I  T  A  L
```

Find and Circle

____ room (five-letter minimum)	○○○○○○○
Four 11-letter words	○○○○
Two five-letter words that mean "hi"	○○
Author King	○
Seek-and-find book series: *Where's ____?*	○
Table, rock, or sea ____	○
Award-winning Kingsley	○
Muppet creator Henson	○

```
V  I  O  L  A  P  S  C  O  D  D
C  Z  C  R  I  E  I  J  V  A  N
E  G  B  L  M  R  N  A  O  E  O
L  I  O  A  E  A  O  T  N  L  B
L  O  J  L  B  V  N  N  L  O  F
O  G  D  Y  D  O  E  L  V  L  L
N  A  Z  U  R  X  U  L  L  A  U
A  C  X  O  L  B  Z  U  A  U  T
G  I  T  J  X  L  P  Z  J  N  E
R  H  E  D  I  T  O  R  S  T  D
O  C  F  U  L  L  D  R  U  M  S
```

Find and Circle

Seven five-letter musical instruments	OOOOOOO
Four four-letter words ending in "ULL"	OOOO
Three large cities on the Great Lakes	OOO
Three four-letter metals	OOO
British secret operative featured in Ian Fleming novels (first/last name)	OO
People who help create puzzle books	O
Seventh sign of the zodiac	O
Uncle's wife	O

233

```
C  B  D  Z  T  N  S  O  F  A  X
G  E  Z  A  W  A  O  K  R  Z  S
B  C  D  A  P  G  B  E  Z  U  A
O  S  P  I  N  P  S  L  C  Z  R
T  I  P  A  G  S  L  R  E  N  M
T  D  M  E  E  I  I  E  O  Z  O
O  H  J  R  A  C  T  M  A  R  I
M  C  D  A  X  C  E  A  L  I  R
A  T  K  Z  B  L  H  D  L  A  E
N  U  G  U  A  V  A  E  E  H  B
K  H  C  O  U  C  H  N  Y  C  C
```

Find and Circle

Nine pieces of furniture	OOOOOOOOO
Five five-letter fruits	OOOOO
DVD: _____ Video _____	OO
The big top	O
Type of cat, or a place to bowl	O
Lowest-ranking chess piece	O
Bear lair	O
Short, quick punch	O

234

```
X Q K E S R E A D S Y
G U L Z S A V D O E T
Z A I E E T I I G E F
T I M E N I T E L I I
N L Y U K O C U A N F
I B X Q C N A Q E G Q
A R Y S I A O U U G U
U I Z Z S L I I Q R E
Q D V X R I D E S O E
R E A L I Z A T I O N
L A M P A E R G U M P
```

Find and Circle

Eight words containing three consecutive vowels (seven-letter max.)	○○○○○○○○
Four 11-letter words	○○○○
Usually the two best-dressed people at a wedding	○○
The square root of 2,500	○
Forrest played by Tom Hanks	○
Whole, skim, or soy ____	○
Tabletop light	○
Poodle or husky, for example	○

235

```
B  J  Z  C  D  D  A  B  E  E  F
E  V  E  E  H  N  I  C  A  L  F
Z  S  E  E  A  E  Z  N  T  X  E
E  E  F  T  U  P  K  E  S  N  R  E
E  P  G  R  E  B  A  S  E  E  T
R  I  I  E  E  F  L  V  E  L  R
F  V  R  N  K  A  I  U  O  D  H
C  C  X  A  K  R  M  C  E  E  C
G  U  E  B  R  O  O  K  X  E  N
V  R  B  S  P  E  E  C  H  P  U
B  K  Y  A  F  L  E  E  C  E  L
```

Find and Circle

Ten words with "EE" in the middle
  ("beet," for example)   OOOOOOOOOO

Four moving bodies of water   OOOO

Three meals   OOO

Two common nursery colors   OO

Tropical American lizard with stout
  legs and a long crest of spines   O

Baby cow   O

Young male horse   O

Four-letter island country   O

```
Y Z C X Y B X Z D V G
A H L Y T Y U A Y N Y
D I O A A U E T I V A
N C W D U R E V T Y D
U K N S B T R S A E I
S O B R F A I D L I R
M K K U C L R L L A F
V W K H C U O I Z Y
K E D T T K B C X T B
X A Z A S T E A K X Y
W K S P A R I N G G C
```

Find and Circle

Six days of a week	○○○○○○
____ knife (five-letter minimum)	○○○○○○
Legendary American frontier scout and marshal: Wild Bill ____	○
Group of birds or sheep	○
Bozo the ____	○
Adult male bovine	○
Dollar nickname	○
Not strong	○

237

```
R  M  Z  B  U  T  T  E  R  X  G
F  O  V  E  N  I  C  E  B  V  T
L  T  M  P  A  U  L  D  O  D  S
O  A  M  E  A  C  E  E  I  E  A
U  S  I  D  X  Z  R  L  L  L  E
R  E  L  E  N  P  U  I  E  B  Y
A  L  A  I  A  E  M  V  D  M  K
B  P  N  R  R  R  M  E  K  A  S
U  A  Z  F  I  U  Y  D  Z  R  A
C  N  P  O  A  C  H  E  D  C  L
S  U  G  A  R  C  H  A  D  S  T
```

Find and Circle

___ eggs (all ending in "ED")	○○○○○
Five common bread ingredients	○○○○○
Four Italian cities	○○○○
Four four-letter countries	○○○○
Card game: gin ___	○
Smallest component of an element having the chemical properties of the element	○
Peter, ___, and Mary	○
Tennis serve that isn't even touched by the opponent	○

```
U S I N G L E R L S Z
M D K I T T E N I L R
P S O Z Z P X H S E A
I O R U A G T J T E I
R U O P B R X T E T N
E T C X O L A R R E E
T H K N V B E K I P L
S Z B T C P S T N O P
E O L O P L S H E C I
W A C E O A O Z O S R
S X P K E T J G X E T
```

Find and Circle

Five six-letter words related to baseball	OOOOO
Four compass directions	OOOO
Four four-letter things worn on the foot	OOOO
Two competing mouthwash brands	OO
Two things commonly found in shakers	OO
Game played with your hands: ____-____-scissors	OO
Two forms of precipitation	OO
Young cat	O

239

```
C Z O K T O F F E E M
J O K F Y J E B V Y A
I Z F L F O U E A A Y
N B U F N E E N E C J
F J A A I F N C E H K
I V C R F N I D C T F
N S X O G F Z A P T F
I U C Z F E E X O E O
T X J O A P R I L X Y
I E K A Y A K X A A A
V L P A Y O F F R S L
```

Find and Circle

Seven six-letter words that contain "OFF"	OOOOOOO
Four five-letter boats	OOOO
Four consecutive months	OOOO
Toyota and Nissan luxury brands	OO
Home to Dallas	O
Fruit commonly grown in Georgia groves	O
Mammal with a white coat: ____ bear	O
The opposite of front	O

240

```
M E D I U M H O U S E
L S C R U B S T Z N H
O R D S P A C E O O E
S O N W X L N X U U R
T V U A J R I X T N O
C I O R O I B H E C E
H V P S G G O S R E S
U R S T A R R U Z B M
C U O B A M A B X O O
K S C L I N T O N Y N
C O P S D E X T E R K
```

Find and Circle

Ten TV shows (four-letter minimum)	OOOOOOOOOO
Three U.S. presidents	OOO
Two five-letter units of weight	OO
Area beyond the Earth's atmosphere: ___ ___	OO
Movie featuring Han Solo and Luke Skywalker: ___ ___	OO
Young male and young female	OO
Batman's sidekick	O
Steady trot just shy of a run	O

241

```
O  S  R  A  M  Z  E  A  L  K  O
L  U  C  K  Z  G  I  I  A  P  N
I  R  V  H  A  L  Z  C  N  E  I
V  E  J  S  E  A  X  H  I  P  O
E  P  U  M  R  E  J  I  T  P  N
S  A  A  B  K  Z  S  L  N  E  S
S  W  I  L  L  I  S  E  E  R  X
K  I  T  C  H  E  N  K  G  S  Y
C  O  L  O  M  B  I  A  R  Z  A
B  A  S  I  L  A  L  G  A  E  D
M  U  S  H  R  O  O  M  S  Z  X
```

Find and Circle

Seven things you might put on a pizza	OOOOOOO
Five South American countries	OOOOO
Soup ____	O
____ Earhart	O
Bruce of *The Sixth Sense*	O
Chlorophyll-containing, mainly aquatic eukaryotic organisms	O
Male sheep	O
24-hour time period	O

242

```
V J B T D S T H Y H H
I O R O I D O S C A G
N H E O N N M A N L U
A N A L E U A C E O O
I N D N R F T T R O D
G A C A O H L A R M B
R I A I R C O C U Y I
E S E L A N V H C R G
T S S A N E A O C R W
T U A T C R R Y I E O
E R R I H F T T T J C
```

Find and Circle

Eight words that mean "money"	OOOOOOOO
Six salad dressings	OOOOOO
Saturday Night Fever star (first/last name)	OO
Animated cat-and-mouse pair	OO
____-____-toe	OO
David who made the puzzle you're playing	O
Female domestic bovine	O
Tom Hanks movie in which he played Josh Baskin	O

243

```
L F R I E D H O T E L L
L V R O A S T E D L E
A H C I V I C K A G T
B L A Z O N E B R R O
T E E N C J T G O I M
E V N B D E Z O T L S
K E O X U B R N O L I
S L T Q X N A E R E N
A E C H O Z N L A D N
B A R A D A R Y L L E
R B A K E D B O N E T
```

Find and Circle

Four sports played on a court	OOOO
____ chicken (all ending in "ED")	OOOO
Four five-letter palindromes	OOOO
Four four-letter words that end with "ONE"	OOOO
Two five-letter lodging options	OO
Cheerios or Wheaties, for example	O
Nickname for a rabbit	O
Reverberation	O

```
O  P  Y  S  P  D  D  D  C  E  E
G  O  D  K  R  E  N  E  A  L  N
N  O  N  U  O  T  O  T  B  C  D
I  L  A  N  V  A  P  A  I  N  O
R  Z  R  K  O  R  V  S  N  U  R
D  R  U  N  K  E  N  N  E  S  S
V  I  N  A  I  G  R  E  T  T  E
G  X  J  R  N  G  L  P  P  N  M
Y  U  T  K  G  A  A  M  A  H  E
B  E  L  T  L  X  K  O  U  O  N
R  V  K  F  Y  E  E  C  L  J  T
```

Find and Circle

Seven 11-letter words	○○○○○○○
Four four-letter bodies of water	○○○○
Three Beatles (first names)	○○○
Word related to a large airplane or a structure you might build in the woods	○
Quaid or Travis	○
Black-and-white member of the weasel family	○
Aunt's husband	○
____ buckle	○

245

```
P A L M A R S M A T E
C C Y W E S T O S Y C
R H M X Z M Y W Y A O
O U M J I R E L M D N
N M U T E N E M M R F
Y R Y T U D S Y E E I
Z T S T A C K N T T D
X Y P R K A Y O R S A
M E M J I N W N Y E N
N O J Z M D A Y Z Y T
C G Y P S Y Y S B U D
```

Find and Circle

Seven words that mean "friend" or "ally"   ○○○○○○○

Seven words that contain two "Y"s   ○○○○○○○

Two planets   ○○

Word with "cotton" or "cane"   ○

The opposite of east   ○

Three-letter bird that comes in a spotted or snowy form   ○

Allen of *Home Improvement*   ○

Cattrall or Basinger   ○

```
M A Y O N N A I S E C
O N I O N X E Z N L H
K Z T J B C K O F E E
F E X O U U C B U G E
L Z T T M A S A S D S
O X T C B A V C I R E
W E J V H Z T H O A K
L R O M E U K O N T F
J A C K A L P A N S O
F I S S I O N R A U X
P I C K L E Z M S M Z
```

Find and Circle

Nine common burger toppings   OOOOOOOOO

Three canines   OOO

Two types of nuclear reactions   OO

Two human appendages   OO

Johann Sebastian ____   O

The capital of Italy   O

Vehicle for transporting students to and from school   O

____ Diego   O

247

```
R O T I N I M Z I T I
L I P A A A M O E X J
I N E L T M A C O I I
N O N P E N I E N L T
G T T P H B A C A O T
U A E H A Z O N C I E
I G B O N D T S H V H
N I D O W N T A I A G
E R N I N A I M M R A
T O R T E L L I N I P
F E T T U C C I N E S
```

Find and Circle

Ten types of pasta	⊙⊙⊙⊙⊙⊙⊙⊙⊙⊙
First three Greek letters	⊙⊙⊙
Two words formed from A-C-E-N-O	⊙⊙
"____. James ____."	⊙
A crossword direction	⊙
One of Christopher Columbus's ships	⊙
Male equivalent of "her"	⊙
Malone played by Ted Danson on *Cheers*	⊙

```
T X N D R Y O Z K N O
O Z O E E A Z N I N S
M J D T F R J L I N S
A O N A U D R M E O Z
T R O N R E A H X W N
O T L I B B T B H A D
H N F M I A M R C R I
C A O U S K I U N S R
N L O L H E L C U A D
I I T L E R E E L W A
Z C L I S B O N Z X M
```

Find and Circle

Six six-letter European capitals	OOOOOO
Four four-letter units of length	OOOO
Three things you're likely to find in salsa	OOO
Two 11-letter words	OO
Lee, Dern, or Willis	O
Midday meal	O
Cookie or cake chef	O
Five-letter type of acid that begins and ends with a vowel	O

249

```
F O R K I M P A L A B
H M A L I B U Z B N R
E D C A M A R O R A O
I F R I N C H E O T N
N Q R E J K T R O T X
E E U I S T J Y K A Z
K G Y E E S X A L H L
E A K V E N I N Y N W
N C R X Z N D N N A O
Z O M E G Z S S G M B
C T A H O E Z C B A R
```

Find and Circle

Five Chevy models	○○○○○
Salad ____	○○○○
Four NYC boroughs	○○○○
Actress whose name is an anagram of "Germany" (first/last name)	○○
A Dutch pale lager	○
Anagram of "finders"	○
One of a yard's 36	○
Nicolas who's the nephew of Francis Ford Coppola	○

```
D E C O R A T I V E Z
E D Z X R F H O R S E
L E X P E R I M E N T
B P K F F A Z E M W O
A A K R E C E N A R T
D R S A R S B U R I U
R T E N E D R L K G L
O M M K N Y A E A H P
F E A Z D O R M B T P
F N H J U L X A L Z O
A T T X M L Z C E X P
```

Find and Circle

Six 10-letter words	○○○○○○
American architect with a distinctive style (first/middle/last name)	○○○
Three five-letter mammals with hooves	○○○
Music made by Britney Spears	○
River that runs through London	○
Long, broad strip of fabric worn about the neck	○
Former planet	○
List of food items that can be ordered	○

SOLUTIONS

Word Roundup Solutions

1 PRINCETON, COLUMBIA, HARVARD, CORNELL, BROWN, YALE—GREEN, TEAL, BLUE, RED, TAN—AUSTRIA, POLAND, FRANCE—MUG, CUP—PEGASUS

....

2 ANDREW, MARTIN, THOMAS, HARRY, JOHN, ABE—VIENNA, BERLIN, BERN, ROME—GRUMPY, SLEEPY—ROCKIES, ALPS—SCRABBLE

....

3 BOTTLE, CRATE, DRUM, JAR, BOX, CAN—MINNESOTA, KENTUCKY, GEORGIA, OHIO—INDIAN, ARCTIC—GARFIELD—NORMAN

....

4 SOMALIA, ANGOLA, EGYPT, CHAD, MALI—TERRIER, SPANIEL, COLLIE—SCORPIO, LIBRA, LEO—CORSICA, CYPRUS, CRETE—HACKMAN

....

5 DRIVER, PUTTER, WEDGE, IRON—KAYAK, KNOCK, KNACK, KICK—LOBSTER, SHRIMP, CRAB—HAMILTON—COLLATERAL

....

6 GARDENIA, AZALEA, TULIP, LILY, ROSE, MUM—VERMONT, MONTANA, MAINE—CHOCOLATE, VANILLA—VERSATILE—JUMANJI

....

7 CAMBODIA, COLOMBIA, CANADA, CHILE, CHINA, CUBA, CHAD—SLEET, SNOW, HAIL, RAIN—SUPERIOR, HURON, ERIE—JOHNSON—ELEVEN

· ·

8 HARMONICA, BANJO, FLUTE, BUGLE, LUTE, DRUM, HARP, OBOE, SAX—AUSTRALIA, AFRICA, ASIA—MOUNTAIN, ISLAND—SAHARA—CANDY

· ·

9 BISHOP, KNIGHT, PAWN, ROOK, KING—ALGERIA, AUSTRIA, ALBANIA, ANGOLA—MONET—UTAH— WHOPPER

· ·

10 BULLDOG, POODLE, BEAGLE, COLLIE, HUSKY, BOXER, HOUND, CHOW, PUG—RINGO, JOHN, PAUL—MORTY— DELAWARE—OHIO

· ·

11 MAGENTA, GRAY, PINK, BLUE, GOLD, TEAL, RED, TAN—TENNIS, SOCCER, RUGBY—THUNDERBALL, MOONRAKER—CANADA—MONTANA

· ·

12 PARSEC, METER, MILE, YARD, INCH, FOOT—MARCH, APRIL, MAY, JUNE—KUDROW, PERRY, COX—ARIZONA— ANGELS

· ·

13 SATURN, VENUS, EARTH, PLUTO, MARS—BRIDGE, RUMMY, POKER, UNO—YESTERDAY, MICHELLE, HELP—HEATON, BOYLE—ALASKA

. . . .

14 LEATHER, COTTON, RAYON, SATIN, SILK, FELT—WYOMING, KANSAS, UTAH—HITCH, ALI—COLGATE, CREST—SCOTLAND

. . . .

15 OREGON, KANSAS, ALASKA, MAINE, IOWA, OHIO, UTAH—CASPIAN, BLACK, NORTH, RED—CLYDESDALE—DANSON—DEPP

. . . .

16 ENGLAND, THAILAND, ICELAND, PANAMA, NORWAY, CUBA—NORTH, WEST, EAST—LISTERINE, SCOPE—BROSNAN—ELF

. . . .

17 LIBERIA, TUNISIA, ANGOLA, EGYPT, CHAD—RUSSIAN, CAESAR, FRENCH, RANCH—MONTH, YEAR, DAY—ISRAEL—EARTH

. . . .

18 SILVER, COPPER, LEAD, GOLD, ZINC, TIN—TIGER, DONKEY, HIPPO, ZEBRA, HORSE, COW—BOISE, BOSTON—PENGUIN—MADRID

. . . .

19 TANGERINE, GRAPEFRUIT, LEMON, LIME—TOYOTA, NISSAN, HONDA, FORD—SPRITE, PEPSI, COKE—TABLE, DESK, BED—DISNEY

. . . .

20 DOLPHIN, WALRUS, WHALE, OTTER, SEAL—OUTBREAK, TOOTSIE, SPHERE—RECTANGLE, CIRCLE, OVAL—ELATION, JOY—GRANT

. . . .

21 COFFEE, WATER, JUICE, BEER, MILK, TEA—SLEET, SNOW, HAIL, RAIN—CHESTER, ANDREW, HARRY, JOHN—RIFLE—DAFFY

. . . .

22 PREPOSITION, ADJECTIVE, VERB, NOUN—MARLINS, ANGELS, TWINS, REDS—CHERRY, APPLE, PEACH—DENVER, DOVER—CENTRAL

. . . .

23 MARYLAND, MONTANA, KANSAS, TEXAS, UTAH—MONDAY, SUNDAY, FRIDAY—CRICKET, MOTH, ANT—BROOKLYN—KERMIT

. . . .

24 JANUARY, OCTOBER, APRIL, JUNE, JULY, MAY—POLAND, FRANCE, GREECE, ITALY—SLIDER, CURVE—SPRING, WINTER—ACURA

. . . .

25 PANTS, SHIRT, SHOES, SOCKS, COAT, BELT, HAT—BOXING, RUGBY, GOLF, POLO—ALBANY, AUSTIN—JEFFERSON—GEORGIA

26 ELEVEN, TWELVE, EIGHT, SEVEN, ZERO, NINE, ONE, TEN, TWO—SHORTSTOP, CATCHER, PITCHER—TRAVOLTA—HOUSTON—BUCK

27 OATMEAL, CEREAL, WAFFLE, BACON, BAGEL, EGGS—HOOVER, NIXON, TAFT, FORD, BUSH—CENTER, FORWARD, GUARD—PENNY, DIME—CANADA

28 ROBIN, GOOSE, FINCH, STORK, DUCK, LARK, SWAN, OWL—TRUCK, JEEP, CAR—GUITAR, BANJO, HARP—MOLLUSK—BARBIE

29 NECTARINE, ORANGE, APPLE, LEMON, PEACH, LIME, PEAR—GERBIL, MOUSE, RAT—POLAND, FRANCE—LIBERACE—HOWARD

30 PANTHER, LEOPARD, COUGAR, TIGER, LION, PUMA, LYNX—ALBERTA, ONTARIO—JAGGER—JACKSON—VERTIGO

31 GROUPER, SNAPPER, SALMON, PERCH, SHARK, TUNA—
THURSDAY, MONDAY, SUNDAY—JOHN, JAMES—HURON,
ERIE—LIVERPOOL

· ·

32 ECUADOR, CANADA, JAPAN, EGYPT, CHILE, NEPAL, PERU,
LAOS, CUBA—LOBSTER, SHRIMP, CRAB—PAUL, JOHN—
LENO—TAXI

· ·

33 MANDOLIN, CLARINET, FLUTE, DRUM, OBOE, TUBA—
NEVADA, OREGON, KANSAS, UTAH, IOWA, OHIO—
PARIS—ELEPHANT—ALPS

· ·

34 APHRODITE, POSEIDON, APOLLO, ZEUS—SOUTH, WEST,
EAST—TABLE, DESK, SOFA—GRISHAM—MATLOCK

· ·

35 GIANTS, BRAVES, CUBS, REDS—ANTARCTICA, EUROPE,
ASIA—PYTHON, COBRA—AMAZON, NILE—THAMES

· ·

36 MAGNOLIA, REDWOOD, SPRUCE, CEDAR, PALM, PINE,
ELM—COYOTE, JACKAL, WOLF, FOX—SATURN, EARTH—
COLUMBO—GOOGLE

· ·

37 FURLONG, METER, INCH, FOOT, MILE—CRICKET, TERMITE,
MOTH, ANT, BEE—VERMONT, MAINE—VENUS—MARS

· ·

38 BOLIVIA, ECUADOR, BRAZIL, CHILE, PERU—WALRUS, WHALE, SEAL—PLATOON, NIXON, JFK—ENGLAND—PACIFIC

. . . .

39 TYLER, GRANT, HAYES, NIXON, ADAMS, FORD, TAFT, POLK— KINGSLEY, AFFLECK, STILLER—DISNEYLAND—ICELAND—GOLF

. . . .

40 SEVEN, NINE, FIVE, FOUR, TEN, ONE, TWO, SIX—SLACKS, SHORTS, JEANS—VIOLET, ROSE—HEAT—GLEASON

. . . .

41 SISTER, FATHER, MOTHER, COUSIN, NIECE, AUNT, SON— AUSTIN, BOSTON, BOISE—PURPLE, INDIGO—GANDHI— PATTON

. . . .

42 NITROGEN, HELIUM, RADON, NEON—SLEET, SNOW, RAIN, HAIL—YACHT, CANOE, ARK—APRIL, JUNE, MAY—RUSSIA, CHINA

. . . .

43 BISHOP, KNIGHT, ROOK, KING, PAWN—SPANISH, ENGLISH, LATIN—SCALLOP, OYSTER, CLAM—NEWMAN—DALLAS

. . . .

44 MOOLAH, BREAD, DOUGH, CASH, LOOT—LAGOON, OCEAN, POND, LAKE, BAY—TENNIS, SOCCER—SPIELBERG— RUSSELL

. . . .

45 CAMEL, HORSE, ZEBRA, WOLF, DEER, GOAT, MULE, COW—MUSKET, PISTOL, RIFLE—EDISON—SCOTLAND—SAJAK

. . . .

46 MERCURY, JUPITER, NEPTUNE, SATURN, VENUS, MARS—MOLOKAI, MAUI, OAHU—KITCHEN, DEN—CHEYENNE—CALICO

. . . .

47 DELAWARE, WYOMING, MONTANA, TEXAS, IDAHO, UTAH—APPLE, PEACH, PEAR, LIME—MARCH, JULY, JUNE, MAY—ACAPULCO—NILE

. . . .

48 LIMBURGER, AMERICAN, ASIAGO, CHEDDAR, SWISS, GOUDA, FETA—MOTH, WASP, ANT, BEE—COSTNER—WEEKEND—HARVARD

. . . .

49 CLASSICAL, GOSPEL, BLUES, JAZZ, ROCK, POP, RAP—SUNDAY, MONDAY, FRIDAY—NORTH, EAST—PENINSULA—SPOCK

. . . .

50 ALBATROSS, CRANE, GOOSE, STORK, SWAN, DUCK, LOON, OWL—TAURUS, ARIES, LIBRA, LEO—NAVY, ARMY—MINNESOTA—DINGO

. . . .

51 VIOLET, WHITE, GREEN, BLUE, CYAN, TAN, RED—ALBANY, PIERRE, SALEM, DOVER—VIOLIN, CELLO, HARP—MONTH, YEAR, DAY—HURON

. . . .

52 MOUSE, HORSE, MOOSE, BEAR, WOLF, LION, DEER, CAT—ROOSEVELT, PIERCE, NIXON, POLK, TAFT, FORD—AFRICA, ASIA—TRANSYLVANIA—COUGAR

. . . .

53 SAXOPHONE, CLARINET, GUITAR, BANJO, FLUTE, OBOE, DRUM—BEAGLE, BOXER, CHOW, PUG—PAMPLONA—CLYDE—PERU

. . . .

54 METER, MILE, INCH, YARD, FOOT—SLEET, SNOW, HAIL, RAIN—IRON, GOLD, LEAD, TIN—VULTURE, EAGLE, HAWK—SUBWAY

. . . .

55 HIBISCUS, AZALEA, DAISY, TULIP, LILY, ROSE, MUM—SPAIN, INDIA, IRAN, CUBA—GERBIL, MOUSE, RAT—ARCHIPELAGO—OTTAWA

. . . .

56 BOXING, HOCKEY, SOCCER, TENNIS, RUGBY, GOLF, POLO—ITALIAN, SWEDISH, ARABIC, FRENCH, LATIN—WALES—RUTH—SEAL

. . . .

57 MAGNOLIA, BIRCH, CEDAR, PALM, PINE, ELM, OAK—
ALLIGATOR, LIZARD, TURTLE, SNAKE—BEIGE, GRAY, RED,
TAN—BROWNELL—JAMES

. . . .

58 CENTURY, SECOND, DECADE, MONTH, YEAR, WEEK,
DAY—TUESDAY, MONDAY, FRIDAY—AMISTAD, MUNICH,
JAWS—SPINACH—NORM

. . . .

59 ELEVEN, THREE, FIFTY, FIVE, NINE, SIX, ONE, TWO—
NICKEL, PENNY, DIME—STEWART, KELLY—SLEUTH—
CRAB

. . . .

60 OCTOBER, MARCH, JUNE, JULY, MAY—BERLIN,
LONDON, PARIS, ROME—PUTTER, DRIVER, IRON—
FLEMING—TEXAS

. . . .

61 APRICOT, ORANGE, CHERRY, PEACH, LEMON, PLUM,
PEAR—DOLLAR, POUND, EURO, PESO—FRENCH, LATIN,
GREEK—MOOSE—CAGE

. . . .

62 MOUNTAIN, CANYON, RAVINE, ISLAND, GORGE,
VALLEY, CLIFF, HILL—TRENTON, DENVER, AUSTIN—VERB,
NOUN—COYOTE—OYSTER

. . . .

63 COLORADO, FLORIDA, ALASKA, KANSAS, MAINE, OHIO—
MAGENTA, CRIMSON, PINK, BLUE, TAN, RED—BROOKLYN—
IMPALA—REINER

. . . .

64 STRAIT, LAGOON, OCEAN, POND, LAKE, GULF, BAY, SEA—
NESMITH, DOLENZ, JONES, TORK—LONDON—WHALE—
CROWE

. . . .

65 MONGOLIA, VIETNAM, INDIA, NEPAL, CHINA, LAOS—
PISCES, TAURUS, VIRGO, ARIES, LIBRA, LEO—OAKLAND—
BOXING—ALDA

. . . .

66 NEPHEW, MOTHER, SISTER, COUSIN, AUNT, SON—MINERVA,
APOLLO, VENUS, MARS—COLUMBUS—GIRAFFE—HOOVER

. . . .

67 TROMBONE, TRUMPET, FIDDLE, BUGLE, DRUM, HARP, OBOE—
KERMIT, ERNIE, GONZO, BERT—BACKUS—JONES—WELLS

. . . .

68 HALIBUT, SALMON, TROUT, SHARK, PIKE, CARP—
SNEAKER, SANDAL, SHOE, SOCK—GRANT, FORD, POLK—
PHILADELPHIA—ROBERTS

. . . .

69 YELLOW, ORANGE, GOLD, TEAL, PINK, TAN, RED—BISHOP,
KNIGHT, PAWN, KING, ROOK—BILLS, BEARS, JETS—
MARTIN—ALASKA

. . . .

70 NITROGEN, NORTHERN, NEUTRON, NATION, NYLON, NEON, NOON, NOUN, NUN—PYTHON, COBRA— FLICK, FILM—TEAL—CUBA

....

71 GOAT, MULE, BAT, PIG, CAT, DOG, RAT, COW—PASTEL, PETALS, PLATES, PLEATS, STAPLE—SMOOCH, PECK— MOMENTUM—PETER

....

72 PENGUIN, PARROT, ORIOLE, ROBIN, LARK, WREN, HAWK, OWL—PUMP, PEEP, PROP, PULP, PIP, PUP, POP, PEP—NORTH, EAST—APRIL, MAY—MARS

....

73 SLEET, SNOW, RAIN, MIST, HAIL—ANNAPOLIS, ATLANTA, ALBANY—CHAIR, DESK, BED—PORKCHOP— TWAIN

....

74 PROVOLONE, PARMESAN, RICOTTA, SWISS, COLBY, BLUE—BATHTUB, BLURB, BLAB, BLOB, BULB, BIB— LEMON—BOONE—CONGO

....

75 CUBA, FIJI, CHAD, LAOS, PERU, TOGO, IRAN—HORNET, MOTH, BEE, ANT—PIANO, TUBA, HARP, OBOE—SUPPER, LUNCH—PORTUGUESE

....

76 KAYAK, YACHT, SKIFF, BARGE, FERRY, CANOE, RAFT, ARK—
HEART, BRAIN, LIVER, LUNG—SACRED, CEDARS, SCARED—
GATES—ZEUS

. . . .

77 FURLONG, PARSEC, METER, INCH, FOOT, MILE, YARD—
BALTIMORE, BOSTON, MIAMI—MONKEY, LEMUR, APE—
EUROPE, ASIA—ARTHUR

. . . .

78 STRAWBERRY, ORANGE, APPLE, MANGO, LEMON, PLUM—
MAGPIE, RAVEN, HERON, WREN, SWAN, LOON—CIVIC,
COMIC, CYNIC—COCOON—BOGGLE

. . . .

79 THIRTEEN, TWELVE, FIFTY, SEVEN, EIGHT, NINE, FOUR, TEN—
COUSIN, AUNT, SON, MOM, DAD—BOLOGNA, SALAMI,
TURKEY, HAM—VERB, NOUN—NIXON

. . . .

80 TRUMAN, MONROE, ADAMS, HAYES, POLK, TAFT, FORD—
WINDOW, WILLOW, WIDOW, WOW—PERIOD, HYPHEN,
COMMA, COLON—POLLOCK—GOLD

. . . .

81 SYCAMORE, HEMLOCK, BIRCH, ASPEN, PALM, ASH, ELM—
HAMMER, WRENCH, PLIERS, DRILL, SAW—BARLEY, MALT,
HOPS—VENUS, MARS—SEATTLE

. . . .

82 SAPPHIRE, DIAMOND, EMERALD, RUBY, OPAL—FIBULA, FEMUR, TIBIA—PISCES, LIBRA, LEO—FORWARD, CENTER— EARP

. . . .

83 AUGUST, MARCH, APRIL, JUNE, JULY, MAY—MANGO, APPLE, PEACH, LIME—SCOTTY, SPOCK, KIRK, SULU— DOUGH, LOOT, CASH—WEST

. . . .

84 DELAWARE, OREGON, KANSAS, OHIO, IOWA—DOLLAR, POUND, PESO, EURO, YEN—DEUCE, KING, JACK, ACE— TANGO, WALTZ, SALSA—JAPAN

. . . .

85 URANIUM, COPPER, IRON, LEAD, TIN—BEAVER, MOUSE, RAT—ROCK, POP, RAP—HURON, ERIE—DOVER

. . . .

86 GLOWING, GIVING, GOING, GONG, GAG, GIG— JAGUAR, TIGER, PUMA, LION—NEAREST, EASTERN, EARNEST—ORANGE, LEMON, LIME—ABDOMEN

. . . .

87 KITTEN, PIGLET, PUPPY, CALF, COLT, CUB—COLONEL, ADMIRAL, PRIVATE, GENERAL, MAJOR—STOP, YIELD— NILE—LOST

. . . .

88 DRESSER, CHAIR, SOFA, BED—SPAIN, CHINA, PERU, LAOS—PACIFIC, CENTRAL, EASTERN—FIBULA, TIBIA, FEMUR—MAINE, OHIO, IOWA

. . . .

89 BERLIN, MOSCOW, LONDON, SEOUL, LIMA, ROME, OSLO—
SLOOP, FERRY, CANOE, RAFT—SAHARA, GOBI—MOOSE—
ETHEL

. . . .

90 AUGUST, APRIL, JUNE, JULY, MAY—ANGELS, TWINS,
METS, CUBS, REDS—HAWAII, ALASKA—VAUGHN—DAFFY

. . . .

91 INDONESIA, NIGERIA, KUWAIT, LIBYA, IRAN—DAISY,
TULIP, LILY, ROSE—TITANIC, ALIENS—CAINE—AMAZON

. . . .

92 VIOLET, INDIGO, ORANGE, YELLOW, GREEN, BLUE, RED—
SILVER, GOLD, LEAD, IRON, ZINC, TIN—ERASER, TWINS—
LIBRA—MACAW

. . . .

93 DOLLAR, RUPEE, RUBLE, FRANC, EURO, PESO, YEN—METER,
INCH, MILE, YARD, FOOT—TRIANGLE, CIRCLE, OVAL—BOND—
NINE

. . . .

94 INLET, OCEAN, LAKE, POND, GULF, SEA, BAY—STRIKE,
SCORE, SPARE, LANE, PIN—LIMPED, DIMPLE—CUBA—
AEROSMITH

. . . .

95 WASHINGTON, HOFFMAN, CROWE, BRODY, PENN, FOXX—
HUTCH, HIGH, HUSH, HASH, HAH—HOLMES—WHALE—
MADONNA

. . . .

96 STORK, GOOSE, ROBIN, CROW, HAWK, OWL—
WITHERSPOON, ROBERTS, THERON, KIDMAN, SWANK,
BERRY—PENNY, DIME—GATES—MALTA

. . . .

97 DEER, BEAR, GOAT, MULE, PUMA, MOLE, LYNX—TRUCK,
JEEP, CAR—SLEET, SNOW, RAIN—FANTASIA, SHREK,
ANTZ—CHICAGO

. . . .

98 TANGERINE, MANGO, APPLE, PEACH, PEAR, LIME—
ALMOND, CASHEW, PECAN—JACKSON, NIXON, POLK—
LUCAS—NOON

. . . .

99 CRICHTON, GRISHAM, TWAIN, STEEL, KING—CARLA,
NORM, SAM—AFRICA, EUROPE, ASIA—PORTUGAL,
FRANCE—BOXING

. . . .

100 CAMBODIA, COLOMBIA, CANADA, CHINA, CHILE,
CUBA—INCISOR, CUSPID, MOLAR—KING, ROOK,
PAWN—DANISH—TITAN

. . . .

Wonderword Solutions

101 Duties	**126** Trainmaster
102 Honest	**127** Stimulating
103 Soldier	**128** Carnival
104 Existentialism	**129** Calendar
105 Entrance	**130** Rolling Pin
106 Anodized	**131** Identification
107 Basket	**132** Birthdays
108 Fascination	**133** Police
109 Wellness	**134** Productions
110 Franchise	**135** Practice
111 Assignment	**136** Karate
112 Walkman	**137** Raptor
113 Jelly	**138** Fireplaces
114 Illuminati	**139** Subdued
115 Garnishes	**140** Fundraiser
116 Repertoires	**141** Paleontologists
117 Trachea	**142** Foundations
118 Conditions	**143** Relics
119 Given	**144** Companionship
120 Flicker	**145** Charity
121 Christmas	**146** Bright
122 Gridlock	**147** Cultivation
123 Talk	**148** Assemble
124 Reservation	**149** Successful
125 Cultivation	**150** Fiction

151 Rhododendrons		**176** Invigorating
152 Passwords		**177** Escargots
153 Pulls		**178** Arrangement
154 Spectacular		**179** Educational
155 Many		**180** Payment
156 Flamboyant		**181** Togetherness
157 Hazardous		**182** Appetizing
158 Old Quarters		**183** Popsicle
159 Virtuosos		**184** Carats
160 Engagements		**185** Convictions
161 Raise		**186** Inevitable
162 Alphabetically		**187** Heritage
163 Masterpieces		**188** Proctors
164 Plunging		**189** Vegetarianism
165 Imagination		**190** Inventory
166 Makeup		**191** Concentration
167 Detention		**192** Mosaic
168 Devour		**193** Restorations
169 Environment		**194** Scallions
170 Adorable		**195** Commissions
171 Passionate		**196** Precious
172 Soothing		**197** Rodeo
173 Collection		**198** Solarium
174 Elizabethan		**199** Benevolence
175 Investigated		**200** Brownies

Word Roundup Challenge Solutions

201 LULLABY, BALLAD, ANTHEM, MELODY, TUNE, HYMN—
LOCAL, VOCAL, DECAY, EXCEL, FOCUS—CHRISTOPHER,
COLUMBUS— HELEN, KELLER—CENTURY—MUSIC—PANDA—
MOLE

. . . .

202 CHANNEL, LAGOON, PUDDLE, HARBOR, OCEAN, LAKE,
POND, GULF, SEA—ZEBRA, ZESTY, ZILCH, ZONES—TOM,
CRUISE—BUTTER, SALT—IRAN, IRAQ—NOVA, SCOTIA—
ALPS—OAK

. . . .

203 YOGURT, BUTTER, CHEESE, CREAM, MILK—SMELT, SHARK,
PERCH, TROUT—FORWARD, CENTER, GUARD—CENTRAL,
EASTERN—HELLO, HOWDY—MADONNA—MATH—TOM

. . . .

204 CLEAR, RAINY, SUNNY, WINDY, HUMID, FOGGY—ROCKIES,
ANDES, ALPS—BOXER, HOUND, HUSKY—MITTENS,
GLOVES—FIELD, HOCKEY—RAY, CHARLES—ADIOS, HOLA—
YAHOO

. . . .

205 PANTHER, CHEETAH, LEOPARD, JAGUAR, COUGAR, TIGER,
PUMA, LYNX, LION—AFRICA, EUROPE, ASIA—KAUAI, OAHU,
MAUI— OPRAH, WINFREY—FRANC—THORN—NECK—ADD

. . . .

206 COLONY, SCHOOL, FLOCK, SWARM, TROOP, HERD, PACK,
POD—CADILLAC, PONTIAC, SATURN, BUICK—LETTUCE,
TOMATO, BACON—BENNY, HILL—SEAN, PENN—BULL—
TOP—TIM

. . . .

207 TERMINATOR, TRANSCRIBE, TECHNICIAN, TELESCOPIC, TECHNOLOGY—TWENTY, FIFTY, FIVE, TEN, ONE—POSEIDON, NEPTUNE—PEPPER, SALT—WILL, SMITH—PUMA—CAVE—RED

. . . .

208 BLOSSOM, JUICE, GROVE, SODA, TREE, PEEL—HEARSE, TAXI, JEEP, VAN, BUS, CAR—MOWER, TOWEL, HOWDY, FEWER, JEWEL—JACKIE, GLEASON—STAIRS—APPLE—GOOSE—CONGO

. . . .

209 BRASILIA, BRUSSELS, BUDAPEST, BEIJING, BOGOTA, BERLIN, BEIRUT, BERN—ARMSTRONG, COLLINS, ALDRIN—CRIME, SCENE—NITROGEN—POODLE—HAND—BLUE—TOE

. . . .

210 WHEATIES, CHEERIOS, MUESLIX, CHEX, TRIX, LIFE—DANUBE, THAMES, RHINE, VOLGA, RHONE—LETTUCE, CHEESE, PICKLE, ONION—LINCOLN—ZEBRA—THOR—PONG—CENT

. . . .

211 OPTOMETRIST, NEUROLOGIST, ONCOLOGIST, PODIATRIST, DENTIST—MALAYSIA, MONGOLIA, MEXICO—FRENCH, POLISH, GERMAN—MUNICH—TOWEL—FOCUS—BUGS—MERV

. . . .

212 PUFFIN, FALCON, CANARY, PARROT, ORIOLE, OSPREY, CONDOR, TURKEY—REVIVE, VALVE, VIVID—PALE, LEAP, PLEA—CONTINUUM, VACUUM—PARAGUAY—FALLS—NOUN—TWO

. . . .

213 FURLONG, METER, INCH, FOOT, YARD, MILE—BLACK, BROWN, BEIGE, BLUE—BLOCKBUSTER, NETFLIX—FRIENDS, FINDERS—BRAD, PITT—SPIDER—HORSE—DEATH

. . . .

214 BARCELONA, MONTREAL, BEIJING, ATLANTA, MUNICH, ATHENS, SYDNEY, SEOUL—COLUMBIA, SYSTEM—COW, PIG—ISAAC—EVEREST—TROPIC—BUCK—AUNT

. . . .

215 UNIFORM, PLAYER, COACH, GLOVE, FIELD, GAME, TEAM, CAP, BAT—MICHIGAN, SUPERIOR, ONTARIO, HURON, ERIE—PERSIAN, SIAMESE—VOLTAIRE—WESTERN—JERRY—LAKE—CHIP

. . . .

216 NUNAVUT, MANITOBA, ALBERTA, ONTARIO, QUEBEC—MUSH-ROOMS, SAUSAGE, PEPPERS, ONIONS, CHEESE—NICKEL, PENNY, DIME—BONNIE, CLYDE—DRACULA—ALLOY—CANOE—TUBA

. . . .

217 GRIME, PRIME, THYME, CHIME, TIME, DIME, LIME, MIME—TWO, FOUR, SIX, EIGHT, TEN— WILLIAM, SHAKESPEARE—MINUTE, HOUR—ALFRED, NOBEL—SNICKERS—SHARK—POLO

. . . .

218 ACCUMULATED, UNDENIABLE, INEVITABLE, CURIOSITY—VANCOUVER, MONTREAL, TORONTO, CALGARY—HERRING, SALMON, MULLET—COUNTY—CANON—MONET—LARVA—PAUL

. . . .

219 DUBLIN, OTTAWA, HAVANA, ATHENS, MOSCOW, LISBON, MADRID, BEIRUT—JURY, JULY, JOLT, JACK, JOKE, JEEP, JAVA—EINSTEIN—ORANGE—PLATO—FISH—BOLT—PEN

220 BEAR, GOAT, MULE, DEER, MOLE, LION, PUMA, WOLF—OCEAN, BAY, SEA—EASTERNMOST, VERTEBRATES—DAVID, LAWRENCE—BRUCE, WAYNE—LIZARDS—YAM—DOVE

221 PANTS, SKIRT, DRESS, PARKA, SHIRT, JEANS, SCARF, WATCH, GLOVE—POULTRY, BEEF, PORK—LIQUID, SOLID, GAS—JACK, QUEEN, KING—BILL, GATES—IVORY—CAB—DAY

222 VIRGO, DINGO, RIGOR, BINGO, AGONY, LINGO, VIGOR, MANGO—DEVELOPMENT, FORTUNATELY, CONVENIENCE, RECTANGULAR—CHEMISTRY, BIOLOGY, PHYSICS—CHUNG—TOM—BOO—ACE—ICE

223 SAFETY, POINTS, HELMET, CENTER, TACKLE, PLAYER, JERSEY, FUMBLE—YOUTHFULLY, YESTERDAY, YEARLY, YUMMY, YUCKY—WHITE, RED—MOUSE—KAYAK—GOLF—BOB—PIG

224 CONCERT, LOBSTER, BOTTOM, GARDEN, CANDY, MUSIC, WALL, BAND, SALT—NEUTRAL, REVERSE, DRIVE—BATMAN, ROBIN—OPAL, RUBY—SCRABBLE—STORK—WING—WAX

225 ARTWORK, BETWEEN, BREWERY, CHEWING, CHOWDER, BROWSER, SEAWEED, SNOWMAN, MEOWING—QUARTER, PENNY, DIME—ORCHARD—CHEERIO—JAMES—NINE—CONE—AMEN

• •

226 MERCURY, VENUS, EARTH, MARS, JUPITER, SATURN, URANUS, NEPTUNE—POLAND, GREECE, SPAIN, ITALY—COLOR, DRYER, BRUSH—AMBULANCE—DOGS—ANCHOVY—CREEK—KEN

• •

227 PAPAYA, RADISH, CHERRY, TOMATO, CARROT, SQUASH, ORANGE, BANANA, PEPPER—ARSON, FLAME, SMOKE—CLYDE, BARROW—TRICYCLE—HARLEM—SUBWAY—REPORT—CAKE

• •

228 SCORPIO, GEMINI, TAURUS, PISCES, VIRGO, LIBRA, ARIES, LEO—MILES, PER, HOUR—DISTRICT, COLUMBIA—SUNRISE, SUNSET—RINGO, STARR—CREDIT—ASIA—WOLF

• •

229 PITCH, COACH, FIELD, GLOVE, CATCH, HOMER—LEMMING, LLAMA, LEMUR, LYNX, LION—SPOON, KNIFE, FORK—JULES, VERNE—ELBOW, KNEE—COWBOYS—MOVIE—POOCH

• •

230 JANUARY, MARCH, APRIL, MAY, JUNE, JULY, AUGUST, OCTOBER, NOVEMBER—SALAMI, TURKEY, HAM—DAISY, LILAC, TULIP—GEORGE, HERBERT—IRAN, IRAQ—RAVEN—PEN—TOP

• •

231 HOSPITAL, WAITING, DINING, LIVING, PANIC, HOTEL, ELBOW—ACCOUNTABLE, CONTINGENCY, ARBITRATION, PREDICTABLE—HELLO, HOWDY—STEPHEN—WALDO—SALT—BEN—JIM

....

232 VIOLA, PIANO, FLUTE, ORGAN, CELLO, BANJO, DRUMS—FULL, BULL, DULL, PULL—CLEVELAND, CHICAGO, TORONTO—GOLD, LEAD, IRON—JAMES, BOND—EDITORS—LIBRA—AUNT

....

233 OTTOMAN, ARMOIRE, DRESSER, HUTCH, TABLE, CHAIR, COUCH, SOFA, BED—GUAVA, PEACH, APPLE, MANGO, LEMON—DIGITAL, DISC—CIRCUS—ALLEY—PAWN—DEN—JAB

....

234 SQUEEZE, SQUEAL, QUAINT, SEEING, QUAIL, QUEEN, QUIET, ADIEU—REALIZATION, AIRSICKNESS, RADIOACTIVE, RATIONALIZE—BRIDE, GROOM—FIFTY—GUMP—MILK—LAMP—DOG

....

235 CHEESE, FLEECE, FREEZE, SPEECH, BEEF, FEED, FEET, DEEP, JEEP, KEEP—STREAM, BROOK, RIVER, CREEK—BREAKFAST, LUNCH, DINNER—BLUE, PINK—IGUANA—CALF—COLT—CUBA

....

236 SUNDAY, MONDAY, TUESDAY, THURSDAY, FRIDAY, SATURDAY—UTILITY, CARVING, BUTTER, PARING, STEAK, BREAD—HICKOK—FLOCK—CLOWN—BULL—BUCK—WEAK

....

237 SCRAMBLED, DEVILED, POACHED, BOILED, FRIED—BUTTER, FLOUR, YEAST, SUGAR, SALT—VENICE, NAPLES, MILAN, ROME—PERU, CHAD, CUBA, IRAN—RUMMY—ATOM—PAUL—ACE

238 SINGLE, DOUBLE, TRIPLE, UMPIRE, BATTER—NORTH, SOUTH, EAST, WEST—SOCK, BOOT, CLOG, SHOE—LISTERINE, SCOPE—PEPPER, SALT—PAPER, ROCK—SLEET, RAIN—KITTEN

239 COFFIN, OFFEND, COFFEE, OFFICE, TOFFEE, LAYOFF, PAYOFF—KAYAK, YACHT, CANOE, BARGE—APRIL, MAY, JUNE, JULY—INFINITI, LEXUS—TEXAS—PEACH—POLAR—BACK

240 SURVIVOR, MEDIUM, DEXTER, HEROES, SCRUBS, HOUSE, CHUCK, LOST, MONK, COPS—CLINTON, BUSH, OBAMA—OUNCE, POUND—OUTER, SPACE—STAR, WARS—GIRL, BOY—ROBIN—JOG

241 MUSHROOMS, SAUSAGE, PEPPERS, ONIONS, CHEESE, OLIVES, BASIL—ARGENTINA, COLOMBIA, BRAZIL, CHILE, PERU—KITCHEN—AMELIA—WILLIS—ALGAE—RAM—DAY

242 CURRENCY, DINERO, MOOLAH, FUNDS, DOUGH, BREAD, CASH, LOOT—VINAIGRETTE, ITALIAN, RUSSIAN, CAESAR, FRENCH, RANCH—JOHN, TRAVOLTA—TOM, JERRY—TIC, TAC—HOYT—COW—BIG

243 RACQUETBALL, BASKETBALL, HANDBALL, TENNIS—
ROASTED, GRILLED, BAKED, FRIED—ROTOR, CIVIC, LEVEL,
RADAR—BONE, TONE, ZONE, GONE—HOTEL, MOTEL—
CEREAL—BUNNY—ECHO

. . . .

244 EXAGGERATED, PROVOKINGLY, RETRIEVABLE,
DRUNKENNESS, COMPENSATED, VINAIGRETTE,
ENDORSEMENT—POOL, LAKE, POND, GULF—RINGO,
JOHN, PAUL—CABIN—RANDY—SKUNK—UNCLE—BELT

. . . .

245 CONFIDANT, COMRADE, CHUM, CRONY, MATE, PAL,
BUD—YESTERDAY, SYMMETRY, SYNONYM, MYSTERY,
SKYWAY, YUMMY, GYPSY—NEPTUNE, MARS—CANDY—
WEST—OWL—TIM—KIM

. . . .

246 MAYONNAISE, LETTUCE, KETCHUP, MUSTARD, CHEESE,
TOMATO, PICKLE, BACON, ONION—JACKAL, WOLF,
FOX—FISSION, FUSION—ARM, LEG—BACH—ROME—
BUS—SAN

. . . .

247 TORTELLINI, FETTUCCINE, MANICOTTI, SPAGHETTI,
LINGUINE, RIGATONI, RAVIOLI, ROTINI, PENNE, ZITI—
ALPHA, BETA, GAMMA—OCEAN, CANOE—BOND—
DOWN—NINA—HIM—SAM

. . . .

248 LONDON, ATHENS, MADRID, LISBON, WARSAW,
BERLIN—INCH, FOOT, YARD, MILE—CILANTRO, TOMATO,
ONION—REFURBISHES, ILLUMINATED—BRUCE—
LUNCH—BAKER—AMINO

. . . .

249 CORVETTE, CAMARO, IMPALA, MALIBU, TAHOE—DRESSING, FORK, BOWL, BAR—MANHATTAN, BROOKLYN, QUEENS, BRONX—MEG, RYAN—HEINEKEN—FRIENDS—INCH—CAGE

••

250 AFFORDABLE, DECORATIVE, DEPARTMENT, REFERENDUM, EXPERIMENT, REMARKABLE—FRANK, LLOYD, WRIGHT— HORSE, CAMEL, ZEBRA—POP—THAMES—SCARF—PLUTO— MENU

••